T0131334

Shimmer, don't Shake

How Publishing Can Embrace AI

Nadim Sadek

Published by Forbes Books, Charleston, South Carolina.
Member of Advantage Media.

Forbes Books is a registered trademark, and the Forbes Books
colophon is a trademark of Forbes Media, LLC.

MENSCH PUBLISHING

Under License from Mensch Publishing
51 Northchurch Road,
London N1 4EE, United Kingdom

First published in Great Britain 2023

A catalogue record for this book is
available from the British Library

ISBN:
979-8-88750-453-7 (paperback)
979-8-88750-454-4 (ebook)

Typeset by Van-garde Imagery, Inc., • van-garde.com

Dedicated to people who stay true
in the face of adversity.

Contents

Prologue

I'm neither a technical expert in Publishing nor in Artificial Intelligence. My focus is on the intersection between them. I've invested time, energy, and my career in understanding how people feel and think, interact with things in the world, relate to brands and other artefacts of human invention, and for the last five years or so, built businesses based on AI. I hold myself out not as prophet nor soothsayer. In this book, I have enjoyed intertwining the histories of Publishing and AI, seeking to understand the most constructive way in which one form of human genius – literature – can benefit from another of its brain-children, machine-learning.

1
A Brief History of
Publishing Innovations

This book is chiefly about artificial intelligence (AI). I want to explore how AI intersects with book publishing. I thought I'd start by looking at how technology has played a part in publishing throughout history, and therefore to be able to contextualise, and give proportion to, the advent of AI and its impact on this long-established industry.

Publishing has evolved dramatically since the earliest days of humanity passing down information through oral traditions and cave paintings. This chapter provides a bird's-eye view of those major innovations that have shaped publishing over centuries leading up to the present day. Subsequently, I'll write a parallel narrative of AI's development, eventually pulling the two histories together.

I find it interesting to look for context around major publishing innovations so I also briefly highlight relevant societal, economic, and political events that were happening concurrently. I'm not a historian and I'm sure many are more expert in this, but I hope that my efforts are in some form enlightening or stimulating. For example, when discussing the advent of the printing press in the 15th century, I noticed how this new technology coincided with the greater trade and urbanisation of that era which fuelled demand for books. Cultural trends at different times also intersected with developments in publishing, such as the pulp fiction boom in the early 20th century. Let me linger for a moment on this, chosen rather randomly, to illustrate how technology affects publishing.

The pulp fiction boom was a period of great popularity for magazines in the United States from the 1920s to the 1950s. Pulp magazines were cheaply-produced and typically featured lurid covers and sensational stories. They were often sold at newsstands and drugstores, and were a popular form of entertainment for people of all ages.

The boom was driven by a number of factors, including the rise of mass literacy, growth of the middle class, and development of new printing technologies. Pulp magazines were also a relatively inexpensive way for publishers to produce and distribute fiction, which made them a popular option for both readers and publishers.

It came to an end in the 1950s as the rise of television and other forms of entertainment began to compete for readers' attention.

The real point is that one technology ushered in an era of specific creativity and publishing, and another technology prompted its demise. It's a repetitive cycle and worth remembering, as one looks at how AI may now also have a great effect on publishing.

My goal is also to give readers a glimpse into the wider historical setting surrounding each transformation in publishing to better understand the life and times. I'm only sketching my way through millennia, for the sake of brevity and to keep to the main narrative around innovation and ultimately AI, but it is fascinating how technology in publishing intersects with wider life. Publishing has always evolved in tandem with the broader forces shaping society and it seems to me that it will remain so, though in much evolved forms.

The Beginnings of Recorded Communication

The evidence is that humans have felt the urge to record stories and information since ancient times. Cave paintings dating back over 40,000 years represent some of the earliest examples of our ancestors communicating symbolically. Oral storytelling also played a central role in early societies, passing down knowledge through generations verbally.

The development of writing systems marked a major transformation around 4000 BC. Sumerians in Mesopotamia began using wedge-shaped symbols pressed into clay tablets, an early form of writing called cuneiform. This enabled literature, business transactions, and other records to be set down permanently for the first time. Imagine the first receipts being on tablets – and then recall that your coffee this morning could well have produced a receipt on another tablet – in some ways, we've barely changed!

Cuneiform and hieroglyphic writing also expanded administrative and commercial activity, as goods and transactions could be catalogued. Rule of law advanced with written legal codes like Hammurabi's regulating society. It's easier to govern when you can point at things written down as the law.

Some of the earliest writings in cuneiform from Mesopotamia recorded important literature like the Epic of Gilgamesh, one of the oldest known works of literature dating back over 4,000 years. Cuneiform was also used to write down daily records, contracts, laws, and other governmental proclamations. For instance, the Code of Hammurabi, which established one of the earliest sets of codified laws in human history, was inscribed on a stone tablet in cuneiform. These examples illustrate how early writing systems allowed societies to document their most important cultural and civic knowledge in permanent records for the first time. We were beginning to live by reference to artefacts, not spoken words and memories.

Hieroglyphics, an elaborate writing system using pictorial symbols, also emerged around 3200 BC in ancient Egypt (as I'm half-Egyptian, I've always found this 'innovation' especially fascinating). This was used for monument inscriptions, correspondence, record keeping, and rituals. Scrolls made of papyrus reeds served as an early flexible format for written works. So, the technology was changing – no longer clay tablets, now we were using bendier ones, easier and cheaper to produce. We were also seeing expendability for the first time – these papyrus documents were not seen as eternally durable.

Hieroglyphics were used to record a wide range of subjects that provide insights into ancient Egyptian society and culture. These included historical records, religious and mythological texts, mathematical treatises, medical manuals, astronomical observations, poetry, and fictional tales. Ancient Egyptian mathematical texts covered areas like fractions, geometry, and algebra. The longer papyrus scrolls, we can now discern, were an early form of books. Did Egyptians 'invent' the book, a series of related sheafs, together telling a story? I'd like to think so.

The ancient Egyptians helped advance writing by moving beyond basic label-like hieroglyphs to using more expressive phonetic signs representing sounds. They developed one of the first cipher alphabets by substituting hieroglyphs for letters. Their pictorial symbols and illuminated manuscript traditions influenced other cultures. Innovations like demotic script and ink on papyrus provided convenient writing mediums. Recording knowledge in enduring formats helped Egyptian learning endure for millennia.

The Phoenicians developed a simplified consonantal alphabet which was widely adopted. Adding vowels, the Greeks created the first major full alphabet that could represent comprehensive speech. Greek writers produced foundational texts on philosophy, drama, history, science, and mathematics that formed the basis of Western thought.

That Phoenician alphabet had an enduring influence which persists into the 21st century. As one of the first phonetic alphabets, it helped set the stage for the widespread adoption of alphabetical writing systems across many cultures. Modern Latin-based alphabets can trace their origins back over 3,000 years to early Phoenician letters. Phoenician seafaring trade also spread writing to new areas. Their invention of ink from tree resin is a precursor to modern ink. Even our numerical system has origins tied to Phoenician numbers. Their pioneering alphabetic accomplishments still shape global literacy and communication.

This would influence other alphabets including the Roman one. The Romans adapted the Phoenician alphabet by adding letters and standardising an official script. Roman scribes and printing innovations helped disseminate Latin writings across their empire. Roman techniques like binding sheets into book forms, parchment pages, and vellum manuscript covers became standards in publishing. Roman square capitals and rustic letter forms influenced classic typeface designs.

We even get the concept of upper and lower case letters from the Romans. The enduring impact of Latin and Roman papermaking and bookbinding methods show their key innovations that still shape publishing. I believe these innovations mark the beginning of industrialisation of publishing, with mass production resulting from new technologies. Words were spreading.

The Game Changer of Printing

Handwritten manuscripts were the norm for recording information for thousands of years until a revolution occurred in the 15th century – the advent of the printing press.

Machines had arrived. This unleashed a tsunami of shared writing.

Through the use of movable type and mechanical presses, books could be mass-produced much more efficiently. This allowed knowledge to spread beyond the elite, to the masses. The printing press changed the game through faster production versus copying by hand, wider distribution of books and ideas, and lower costs making printed material more accessible.

Key innovators like Johannes Gutenberg played a pivotal role in this global shift. He was a blacksmith and businessman who conceived the idea of the printing press and movable type cast from metal in the 1430s. His machine consisted of a hand mould for casting individual letters, a metal alloy with tin and lead, and a wooden screw-type printing press based on wine presses. The movable type letters were arranged into sentences and paragraphs, inked, and then pressed onto paper. This standardised system allowed pages to be reproduced quickly and efficiently.

Gutenberg's landmark 42-line bible was the first major book printed in Europe using his revolutionary technology. By 1470, over twenty million volumes had been printed. We are so inured to big numbers these days that I do invite you to pause and contemplate that one for a second. Twenty million! Before that, we just had a few sheaves of hand-written things piled together. We are recording this point as the start of a rapid spread of printing across the continent. This physical machinery replaced handwritten manuscripts and launched knowledge distribution on a massive new scale. Distribution! This is also a new concept taking flight. Copies of things could be shared, in great volumes. This set the stage for printing to proliferate rapidly across Europe and beyond.

As I'm writing in London, it's worth pausing to reflect on William Caxton who was the first English printer and published the first printed book in English, *Recuyell of the Historyes of Troye*, in 1473. He set up England's first printing press in Westminster and printed over a hundred books before his death in 1492, playing a key role in localising publishing and spreading literature in the English vernacular. Caxton adapted printing methods for English characters and established the first English press for end-to-end book production, helping grow English literature identity. Book Production! Another concept in its infancy. We are so used to books surrounding us now, but imagine, before this time, you would not see them everywhere. The world literally looked different before Gutenberg and Caxton.

Caxton also handled the entire book production process locally rather than relying on imports. This localisation of publishing helped printing spread through England and aided the growth of literature in English. In a sense, Caxton demonstrated an early example of sustainable, in-country publishing. It's but a faint harbinger of today's sustainability agenda, but it's there.

Two steps back, three steps forward, now. *The Epic of Gilgamesh* from ancient Mesopotamia is considered one of the earliest known works of literature, dating back over 4000 years. Early versions were inscribed on clay tablets. Much later, it was among the first literary works committed to a printing press by publishers who saw the new technology as a way to make such classics more widely accessible. This pattern of adopting the printing press to preserve and spread treasured texts catalysed publishing. Technology was revivifying things lost in time. (Today, we know things 'live forever on the internet' ... and AI's role in permanence is interesting, not just in re-exposing works lost from common attention, but also in distilling their 'DNA' so that the modern, information-saturated mind, can grasp and process important themes from different eras.)

This pattern was mirrored with Gutenberg's Bible being among the first major printed books. In both cases, the new technology of printing was embraced as a way to make foundational texts more permanent, reproducible, and accessible after being preserved for so long in fragile formats. Just as *Gilgamesh* was elevated from scattered tablets to unified books, Gutenberg and Caxton transformed how the Bible and other classics could be studied, saving fragile manuscripts from overuse. The canonical nature of these works inspired early publishers to adopt print. 'Permanence of thought and creativity' had arrived as a notion.

Aldus Manutius in Venice was a key figure in the early evolution of book printing, driving many innovations that improved accessibility. His portable, affordable pocket editions printed with his new italic type represented an early disruption, bringing knowledge to common people. Manutius' small italic allowed the first pocket-sized books, making knowledge during the Renaissance more accessible as literacy grew. So, we now had iteration ... technology going from v1 to v2 to v3.3.1 and so on ...

and with it, new markets and use-cases arising. Here we see the start of mass-marketing.

This allowed more affordable access to knowledge as literacy grew during the Renaissance through expanded education and reading material availability. Manutius' contributions built momentum during a crucial period when printing was still new and evolving rapidly. Much as smartphones combined incremental innovations, printing capabilities exploded in the fifty years after Gutenberg thanks to improvements by publishers like Manutius that compounded the spread of knowledge.

Early printing houses sprung up in major cities across Europe in the late 15th and early 16th centuries. The printing press played a pivotal role in the Renaissance movement by enabling texts and new ideas to be disseminated widely to scholars, artists, religious reformers, and the public.

The Renaissance was defined by a spirit of humanism, invention, and openness to disruptive new ideas. It embraced innovations like printing and the scientific method which upended traditional knowledge distribution and truths.

Book Publishing was a fundamental industry of the Renaissance.

Perfecting the Printing Process

In subsequent centuries, incremental innovations incrementally improved the printing process. Advances like steam power, linotype machines, offset printing, and photocomposition made printing faster and more cost-effective. It's the same as the micro-wave in your kitchen, or your car having anti-lock brakes.

With each there was a sense of wonderment at how things were improving, just as there often is today. The waves of printing innovations evoke comparisons to the rapid evolution of smart-phones over the past decade or so.

Just as steam power and linotype transformed printing in the 1800s, smartphones have seen continuous advances from 3G to 4G to 5G networks, more powerful processors, better displays and cameras, and new capabilities like mobile payments, finger-print sensors, and facial recognition. Each new feature creates wonderment at the pace of change. It also allows new use-cases.

The introduction of stereotyping in the early 1800s allowed reusable plates to be created from composed type. This sped up future reprints so new typesetting wasn't required each time. Steam power and the rotary printing press arrived in the 1810s and massively increased efficiency by mechanising printing on a rolling cylinder rather than pressing flat sheets manually. Volume-efficiency had arrived.

The linotype machine developed in the late 1800s revolu-tionised typesetting by automating it through a line-casting de-vice. Operators used a 90-character keyboard to set entire lines which were assembled into metal casts used for printing plates. This sped up composition significantly.

In the 20th century, offset printing further improved speed and quality. The evolution of printing technology across con-secutive innovations echoes the rapid development of mobile phones over generations. Books were part of life, and they became cheaper, more accessible, more widely distributed, and more varied in nature.

Just as linotype automated typesetting, smartphones introduced touchscreens, cameras, and internet connectivity that revolutionised functionality. Both lineages show how once a foundational technology is established, continuous improvements compound capabilities rapidly.

This period of printing innovation coincided with major changes like the Industrial Revolution, urbanisation, expansion of public education, improved transportation networks, and the rise of consumer culture. As printing capabilities improved, books and newspapers could spread information faster reflecting wider trends. Political debates also proliferated with cheaper printing. Publishing advances both impacted and mirrored their rapidly changing times.

Mass printing enabled the explosive growth of newspapers and serialised fiction in magazines. Works were issued episodically to build readership and suspense. Affordable books, newspapers, and magazines catered reading material to a growing middle class.

New formats and applications of technology were opening up new markets – like that pulp fiction example I mentioned at the start of this chapter.

Impact of Printing Technology on Literacy and Education

The printing press made it possible to produce books and other printed materials more cheaply and efficiently than ever before. This led to a dramatic increase in the availability of books, which in turn helped to fuel the growth of literacy. In the centuries following the invention of the printing press, literacy rates soared across Europe and the Americas. This had a profound impact on education, as it made it possible for more people to access educational materials and to learn to read and write. Information, thought, and creativity were being democratised.

The printing press also helped to democratise knowledge and wisdom. Prior to the invention of the printing press, knowledge was largely controlled by the elite. Only wealthy individuals and institutions could afford to own books, and these books were often written in Latin, which was a language that only the educated elite could understand.

The printing press made it possible to produce books in vernacular languages for a much wider audience. This helped to spread knowledge to people from all walks of life, and it contributed to the development of a more informed and educated citizenry.

So, technology enabled publishing and publishing enabled intellectual power in much broader swathes of society.

Impact of Printing Technology on the Development of New Ideas and the Spread of Dissent

The printing press made it possible for people to share their ideas with a wider audience. This could lead to challenges to the status quo, as people could now spread their ideas more easily and widely. For example, the printing press played a role in the Protestant Reformation, as it allowed Martin Luther to spread his ideas to a wide audience. The printing press also played a role in the American Revolution, as it allowed Thomas Jefferson and other revolutionaries to spread their ideas about liberty and democracy. One might say, the rabble was being roused.

The printing press has had a profound impact on the development of new ideas and the spread of dissent. It has made it possible for people to share their ideas with a wider audience, and this has helped to shape the course of history. Look to China and the Little Red Book ... different figures with different thoughts were alighting upon the power of a published set of written words to educate, illuminate, subjugate, alienate, and everything else that we, as humans, do to each other.

The book was becoming an extension of an individual, a tool by which to share and impress others.

Arrival of the Digital Era

A pivotal transition began in 1971 with the birth of 'Project Gutenberg' which made books electronically available for the first time by manually typing and formatting texts. Founded by Michael Hart, it was a landmark effort to digitise texts and make them available electronically. Clay tablets became papyrus that became sheafs of paper and then bound books ... and now, their physical form was morphing into the new medium of the day: Zeros and Ones electronically arranged by computers.

Volunteers manually typed works which were then proofread and formatted with markup tags before being posted online. This paved the way for digitally storing and distributing literature.

The invention of the personal computer in the 1970s and 1980s brought major changes. Suddenly individuals had affordable technology capable of assisting with writing and designing page layouts. IBM introduced the first personal computer. Programs like PageMaker enabled authors to format works directly on PCs. By 1985, desktop publishing allowed users to design, typeset, and print materials on a PC. Digital books soon followed with Project Gutenberg ebooks and later Amazon's Kindle. Information was becoming instantly accessible from anywhere. These digital capabilities connected people across geography as information became instantly accessible globally.

To access all of humanity's ingenuity and creativity, you didn't even need a computer now – just a device that worked those Zeros and Ones back into words for you. And they became cheaper and ever more simple to use. The digital era has become the start of the disintermediation of those who make physical artefacts of books, and the start also of the content being king.

Wider digital transformations happening concurrently included growth of the internet and email, ecommerce sites like eBay and Amazon, instant messaging, ATMs and digital banking, as well as new technologies like CDs and DVDs. Across industries like media, finance, and communications, digital capabilities were revolutionising operations and business models. Society was moving towards always-on connectivity and instant information access.

One can pause to wonder whether our intellectual faculties had really had a chance to evolve and catch up with the shift from an oral tradition of a few stories being told by a few people, to information of all sorts being endlessly present and available in unfathomable scale.

Amazon's 2007 Kindle device and ebook format sparked major growth in digital books. Over time, physical book sales have been locked in stiff competition with ebooks that offered convenience and portability. Brick-and-mortar bookstores have faced growing struggles competing with online retailers. Self-publishing grew easier with print-on-demand services like Amazon's CreateSpace, IngramSpark, Barnes & Noble Press, Lulu, Blurb, Smashwords, and Reedsy. Ebooks provided a new path for authors to self-publish without traditional publisher gatekeepers. Authors can often distribute to multiple channels like bookstores, libraries, websites, and can customise options like trim sizes, paperback or hardcover, and binding styles.

So, publishers and editors (benevolent censors in one interpretation) were also being disintermediated. You could now say what you want and use an amplifier to reach more eyes and ears than ever before.

While ebooks and online bookselling were disrupting traditional publishing, new opportunities also arose to leverage digital capabilities. Data analytics informed targeted marketing. Social media created new reader communities. Digital printing enabled cost-effective shorter print runs. Audiobooks and virtual reality technology brought new ways to experience content.

The Epic of Gilgamesh would today be presented in a kaleidoscope of formats, each equipped to suit a particular psychological profile, and predilection of taste in a reader. Human genius can flourish like never before.

Current Key Innovations in 2023

It strikes me that a few of these things will characterise innovation in 2023, when I'm writing.

Artificial intelligence is enabling more automated content generation using natural language models. This can help publishers produce customised marketing materials and descriptions more efficiently. AI sales forecasting tools also leverage reader data to predict future demand patterns and make data-driven publishing decisions.

Publishers offer digital subscriptions for access to curated collections of ebooks. Personalised reading apps like Scribd analyse individual preferences to recommend relevant titles and authors. These digital delivery models provide tailored reading experiences.

Social networks have created direct engagement opportunities between authors, publishers, and readers. Platforms like Goodreads and TikTok enable book discovery through sharing reviews, recommendations, and exclusive content. Virtual events connect creators and fans.

Immersive audiobooks read by voice actors are surging in popularity. Podcasts like *Books on the Nightstand* offer author interviews and book discussions. The audio format expands books' reach and resonance.

Emerging digital enhancements like animated illustrations and augmented reality bring stories to life visually. Interactive children's books integrate games and activities. These innovations create multi-media reading adventures.

'Book-vergence' integrates text, video, audio, and graphics into unified multimedia experiences. Enhanced ebooks allow embedded author commentary and interviews. Transmedia storytelling expands narratives across platforms.

Reader analytics inform data-driven publishing, customising content based on preferences and engagement data. Strategic adaptation of books to optimise resonance relies on insights extracted from user behaviours.

Print-on-demand eliminates the risk of overprinting physical copies. Instant ebook delivery removes fulfilment and shipping costs. Streamlined distribution innovations maximise publisher flexibility and customer convenience.

The publishing industry continues to harness emerging technologies while retaining the essence of connecting authors and audiences.

Looking Ahead

Publishing has undergone an incredible evolution from oral histories told around fires to billions of ebooks (and even more many-splendoured versions) available at one's fingertips. The quest to record and share information and creative works has propelled innovations across centuries, with the common thread of striving to reach broader audiences.

As digital capabilities grow more sophisticated, publishers continue adapting to new technologies while staying grounded in their essential role – amplifying authors' voices and ideas that enrich our world.

Artificial intelligence promises to be the next major innovation reshaping publishing. As AI capabilities advance, industry practitioners have legitimate concerns but also much opportunity. I'll discuss these more in subsequent chapters.

While publishing is still in the early stages of leveraging AI, many other industries are seeing it revolutionise workflows. AI powers fraud detection in finance, predictive maintenance in manufacturing, personalised recommendations in retail, automated vehicles in transportation, and medical diagnosis.

Core and fundamental human creativity and ingenuity remain irreplaceable. Book publishing can thoughtfully adopt AI technologies while ensuring they complement, not replace, the imaginations of authors and others in the publishing industry. Publishers who balance AI's benefits while respecting the human need for originality will see it uplift, not undermine, the core mission of disseminating knowledge and sharing genius

2
A Brief History of AI Innovations

Where did all this AI come from, then?

As usual with phenomena we become 'suddenly' aware of, there has been a long gestation. I thought we'd whip through time and see where some of AI's DNA was laid down.

Since ancient times, humans have sought to instil machines with intelligence – from automata to today's digital assistants. Let's pause on automata, because I think that's still what lurks under the surface of our fascination with, and dread of, AI.

Google's English dictionary is provided by Oxford Languages and defines Automata as moving mechanical devices made in imitation of a human being, or, machines which perform a range of functions according to a predetermined set of coded instructions. Automata somehow resemble us.

We seem to find it inherently 'un-natural' to have a facsimile of ourselves. It's unsettling, deranging. We are wired to recognise patterns and to learn to attribute sets of characteristics to particular entities. A machine that behaves like us is conceptually difficult to handle.

AI is weird for us. It's like us in too many ways to be diminished as a mere machine, yet we can't figure out where or how or why it can seem so like us. And because it's not andromorphic, we can't even really 'see' it. There are no eyes to read, no body language to figure out. Largely, it messages us now, and we all do a lot of that, but usually we 'see' the person talking to us. With AI, we can't quite figure out the nature of our correspondent.

It's hidden in swirls of strange terms and concepts that we keep needing to learn anew. Yet, even if we do this assiduously, still AI shape-shifts around us, developing from birth to adulthood with an uncanny pace.

We've to get to some form of identification, to have any chance of achieving comfort with it. So, let's try now.

This chapter traces major milestones chronologically turning 'thinking machines' from speculation into reality. They end up being AI. We'll see how society greeted each advancement with a mix of wonder and trepidation. And we'll get to where we are today, knowing we have a new presence in our midst, yet not sure we welcome them or know quite how to interact with them.

Precursors to AI: Mathematics, Computation, and Automata

Long before artificial intelligence emerged, humans sought to mechanise intelligence through generations of mathematical and computational advances.

The formalisation of mathematics and geometric proofs by scholars like Euclid was largely embraced in intellectual circles. It was difficult stuff to get your head around. The logical deductive reasoning underpinning mathematical advances was admired by academics and philosophers. The abstract nature of theoretical mathematics was, however, obscure to the average citizen. That still sounds familiar about AI today.

Applied mathematics for purposes like accounting, navigation, and astronomy gained more practical appreciation as it demonstrated tangible benefits, grounding it in everyday benefits. There's a lesson there – when things are useful, we tend to like them better. But systematic mathematical thought was treated with scepticism outside of intellectual establishments. Just like AI, it felt very present but simultaneously indecipherable.

Calculating tools such as the abacus also evolved over centuries as civilisations sought to mechanise rote mathematical tasks. Adoption of these early calculating aids was gradual, initially limited to merchants applying them for trade and finance. That usefulness lesson again. Give me something that makes my work better, faster, less onerous, higher quality, more rewarded, more prestigious, and I'll like it better.

As tools like John Napier's logarithms and mechanical adding machines were introduced, they faced some resistance. But computational automation found wider acceptance as it proved advantages in business, science, navigation, and accounting. We could travel better, trade better, and learn better. Better is good.

Of course, mechanical calculation was treated with a mix of wonder and wariness, as some worried such tools could replace human effort. There comes a point with an innovation where it's just too clear to too many that it helps us all, for us to rail against it. Does anyone today resent a pocket calculator?

Inventors also sought to mechanise intelligence by creating automata that could perform functions, like writing, through intricate clockwork mechanisms. Al-Jazari's early 12th century automata, powered by water, dazzled, and entertained onlookers. Contemporary Islamic scholars questioned the frivolity of such mechanical amusements. That didn't really last long though.

Although he didn't specifically create a humanoid automaton, his *Book of Knowledge of Ingenious Mechanical Devices* showcased various mechanical marvels. One notable creation was the water-powered 'Musical Boat', featuring humanoid figures playing instruments. Al-Jazari's work influenced future inventions, and while direct lineage is challenging to establish, his ideas contributed to the development of modern devices such as robotics, automated musical instruments, and complex mechanical systems. Would we have a TV without his precursive work?

People at the time weren't sure about his devices, but though the concept of automated writing machines emerged much later in history, they built upon the foundation of mechanical engineering and invention established by pioneers like Al-Jazari. What we initially recoil from, we often ultimately embrace.

When 18th century figures like Jacques de Vaucanson and Pierre Jaquet-Droz created automata that could draw, play music, or write, the lifelike machines stirred both marvel and discomfort. As clockwork animatronics became more common in Europe, the public expressed a blend of fascination and unease. The automated creatures' humanlike appearance and movements made many wary that they could replace or deceive people.

All the same, their ground-breaking work laid the foundation for modern technologies. Vaucanson's automated loom contributed to industrial automation, while Jaquet-Droz's programmable automata dolls influenced the development of programmable machines and early computers. A playful doll, amusing us in the 18th century seems to have laid the foundations for me to be writing this on my laptop. Who'd have thought that would happen? Should we try harder to appreciate the true consequence of an innovation, as it arrives in our midst, rather than waiting for life to prove it worthwhile?

Expertise in mechanical engineering and watchmaking shaped the fields of robotics, animatronics, and precision timekeeping. Today, their legacy can be seen in industrial robots, automated manufacturing systems, advanced robotic technologies, and the intricate complications found in mechanical watches.

These pillars of mathematics, computation, and early efforts at mechanisation established conceptual and technical foundations that enabled the eventual emergence of artificial intelligence. The synthesis of number-crunching digital computing with higher-order pursuits like logic, language, and creativity built upon centuries of preceding developments aimed at mechanising intelligence.

Our lives are surrounded by innovations the full impact of which we often cannot contemporaneously conceive. More simply, we just don't get it a lot of the time. The challenge now, is for us to try to 'get it' while it's happening around us.

Early Exploration Into 'Thinking Machines'

It wasn't until the mid-20th century that serious research into 'thinking machines' emerged.

In 1943, Warren McCulloch and Walter Pitts modelled the first artificial neurons, laying foundations for neural networks. We knew quite a lot about our brains and thought imitation could be productive.

They presented neurons as simple binary threshold logic units. When combined in networks, these models exhibited problem-solving abilities demonstrating the potential for emergent intelligence through interconnected neuron-like nodes. This breakthrough spawned new recognition that brains and computers could hold similarities at a fundamental level. Though rudimentary, these conceptual artificial neurons and networks kindled hopes that human-made machines could one day exhibit capabilities akin to biological cognition. We were playing with re-creating ourselves, at least in neurological terms.

Alan Turing's 1950 paper introduced his famous Turing Test for measuring machine intelligence. Turing proposed an 'imitation game' where a human evaluator interacts with a computer and a human respondent through text alone. If the evaluator can't reliably distinguish between them, the computer is deemed to have exhibited intelligence comparable to a human's.

This elegantly simple thought experiment proposed behavioural aptitude as the benchmark for intelligence. Rather than just focusing on mechanising mental processes, Turing helped formalise the pursuit of machines that could emulate and engage with people as intellectual equals. The philosophically provocative concept stirred both excitement about the possibilities and unease about human identity. We're still squirming.

We are fascinated by our 'innate' ability to distinguish between truths and falsehoods, to know right from wrong, to decide if something is real or fake. So, we made it into a fundamental test that machines must pass. And now they do! Why did we want to do this? And now that they can exhibit human verisimilitude, why are some of us feeling so uncomfortable (about something we set out to achieve)? I know, we didn't all ask for this to be produced and some of us feel it's been foisted upon us without our invitation or consent. We're prickling.

The 1956 Dartmouth Conference convened pioneering researchers interested in creating thinking machines. Attended by figures like John McCarthy, Marvin Minsky, and Claude Shannon, this gathering marked the official formation of artificial intelligence as a research discipline. Their proposal not only coined the term 'AI' but expressed aspirations such as making machines exhibit creativity and language comprehension. That was just 67 years ago (as I write in 2023).

Over the past 67 years, major events and developments have shaped our world. The Cold War and subsequent fall of the Soviet Union marked a significant geopolitical shift. The civil rights movement fought for racial equality. Space exploration expanded our understanding of the universe. Technological advances, including the internet and smartphones, transformed communication, and connectivity. Global conflicts, such as the Vietnam War and ongoing Middle East conflicts, have had a lasting impact. Medical breakthroughs, environmental concerns, social movements for equality, and the digital revolution have also played crucial roles in shaping our modern society. Meanwhile, we've been trying to make machines exhibit human-like intelligence and doing rather well at that.

Dartmouth signalled unified, scientific dedication to achieving the seemingly impossible – intelligent computers. It also raised anxieties over whether mechanising human traits was prudent or possible. The gathering set lofty goals for the new field, while highlighting the tension between scientific curiosity and ethical concerns regarding human-like AI.

They persist today. We've more or less achieved what was set out as an ambition, without yet resolving how we should feel about the thing we set out to do – the technical objective has been largely proven as achievable, but the ethical concerns are far less addressed.

Teaching Computers to Learn

In the 1950s, most AI relied on rigid rules laboriously hand-coded by programmers. A breakthrough emerged in 1959 when Arthur Samuel created a checkers-playing program that could improve through experience. Rather than hard-coding checkers strategies, Samuel's program refined its play by competing against itself and learning from wins and losses. This machine learning approach, where software optimises based on data instead of fixed rules, demonstrated that computers could exhibit fluid intelligence more like humans. We were teaching a machine to understand how to do better. That's pretty much the foundational thought in human education.

Samuel coined the term 'machine learning' and continued pioneering approaches allowing computers to independently adapt based on information. The conceptual leap of 'learning' over 'programming' opened new possibilities for more capable AI. How often has one human said to another, 'can you try to figure that out for yourself, please'? Well, we have treated computers the same way...

Sceptics argue that true intelligence requires deeper understanding beyond pattern recognition in data. And so we decided to make it more nuanced and 'smart'. Once again, we looked within ourselves, especially at our brains.

Neural networks took inspiration from biology, composed of interconnected processing nodes akin to neurons. Ingeniously, by adjusting the signalling strength between nodes, neural nets could 'learn' based on training data without explicit programming. The more data patterns the network was exposed to, the more adept it became, like humans master things through practice. While biologically inspired, early neural nets were rudimentary, fuelling excitement about human-like learning but producing limited practical impact. The important thing was, they showed a paradigm shift from rules-based to learning-based AI.

Geoffrey Hinton's breakthrough 'backpropagation' algorithm allowed neural networks to be trained with far more layers by correcting errors iteratively through the network. This multi-layer architecture constituted 'deep learning', which along with abundant data and GPU (Graphics Processing Units) processing power, catapulted neural networks from obscurity to revolutionary mainstream methods. It was all getting smarter and smarter – like we humans do, as we gradually learn to involve more and more of our intellectual processing capacity. AI had left elementary school and was headed for high school.

By learning hierarchical representations from raw data, deep learning achieved remarkable results across domains such as image and speech recognition, previously thought to be insurmountable in prior iterations of AI. But its lack of transparency about how it was working and achieving its results fuelled unease that neural networks could act unpredictably or be used nefariously. AI had discovered the power of human-like skill acquisition, but darker societal implications lurked beneath the surface. Adolescence was looking difficult.

The AI Winter Thaws

Most early AI systems disappointingly failed to live up to promises, leading to collapsed funding and diminished interest dubbed 'AI winters'.

Then, in 1997, IBM's Deep Blue defeated world chess champion Garry Kasparov using traditional rules-based AI. Though lacking deeper intelligence, Deep Blue's victory within the complex game revived mainstream interest in human-competitive AI.

We are prone to being drawn to dramatic events of an unusual nature, even if they're really not 'the main event'. As I write, OceanGate's Titan submersible has just generated weeks of global media coverage, as it presented a small thing pitted against a huge one. Meanwhile, the world witnessed little of a migrant boat with roughly 700 people being lost in the Mediterranean.

Deep Blue drew us to its dramatic victory because it was, dramatic. AI learns that it's that sort of thing that draws our attention and can learn to give us what we like. It's akin to conditioning a dog to stop doing silly things and do desired things instead. So, ahead of us lies quite a lot of reflection on the human condition, as we create a phenomenally powerful new collaborator and companion on our journey through civilisation. How do we reward its learning? In which directions should we encourage it?

While not representing true advancement, Deep Blue's theatrical human versus machine competition demonstrated AI's potential to the public. With renewed funding and data-powered methods on the horizon, AI's long winter was finally thawing.

In the 2000s, machine learning quietly gained traction without fanfare in specialised applications like credit card fraud detection. It was busy reducing remarkably labyrinthine data problems into pretty mundane solutions that we would quickly come to take for granted. But the computing capabilities to catalyse its explosion were just around the corner.

When cloud computing unlocked virtually limitless data storage and GPUs provided massive processing power, AI's spring blossomed. Deep neural networks were especially ripe to capitalise on this new-found data and computing bounty. The stage was set for the coming series of revolutionary leaps in practical AI. It had developed its pre-fontal cortex and was ready to go into tertiary education.

The Rise of Modern AI

Everything changed in 2012 when a large neural network called AlexNet soundly defeated rivals in an image recognition challenge after being trained on GPU-accelerated deep learning.

Practically overnight AI was thrust back into the public spotlight. With abundant data and computing resources, deep learning achieved remarkable accuracies on previously impenetrable problems like image classification. Remember the thrill of curating your contacts list on your first cellular phone? AI was suddenly taking our images and sorting them out with inconceivable orderliness. It felt like magic.

Silicon Valley giants began aggressively pursuing AI, building it into consumer products like Apple's Siri. Investment and interest exploded as AI became embedded in numerous industries. Concerns also emerged about potential misuse and the technology's inscrutable decision-making. Innovation was causing delight and suspicion. It was ever thus.

In 2015, Google's AlphaGo defeated the world champion at the ancient game of Go using reinforcement learning, in which trial-and-error gameplay honed its skills. Mastering Go's intuitive strategy was considered an insurmountable task for AI just years earlier. AI had graduated and was pursuing its Master's degree.

This superhuman domination of such a complex and creative game marked a milestone in AI's evolution. It demonstrated how human-like learning could push AI beyond narrow applications into arenas demanding more general intelligence. While exciting, AlphaGo stirred unease about the implications of thinking machines exceeding human capabilities. This theme never goes away.

It seems we have a concern about control. When we're in control, we're more comfortable. When we might be superseded, countermanded, or opposed, we are less easy, especially if our collaborator conceptually remains in our mind as our servant, not our master. It is this existential tension with AI that appears most to challenge our tranquillity around embracing it as a new beneficent force in civilisation.

Ongoing advances in natural language processing models like Google's BERT and Open AI's GPT-series now allow AI to generate remarkably human-like text. These are 'Foundation' or 'Large Language Models' enabling us all to accelerate our learning at break-neck speed. If you have ever felt the thrill of asking a schoolmate for the answer to something you couldn't, or were too lazy to, figure out, you'll understand how it can feel finally to be able to interact with the remarkable capability of AI. It was ChatGPT that simply urged us to us, 'just ask' and suddenly we were thrilled and seduced into doing so endlessly. It's like the Nike of AI – branded, clean, and easy, making you feel positive.

Suddenly, we can feel that the only limitation to what we can find out about, is our ability to conceive a good question. This excites us. We feel that 'better' thing again – I can do better with this ... I like it.

There are rules about this relationship we oddly must learn, but we're doing so quickly. Don't trust everything AI says. Remember it hallucinates. Get another opinion. It's as if the now-PhD student is simultaneously wizardly-brilliant, yet prone to errancy, deception and unreliability. It's a tricky dynamic we humans have got ourselves into, having created our longed-for supermate. How much can we trust it? To what extent is it reliable?

Notice how AI has done something really fundamental? It's moved from calculating, to communicating. That's so much easier for us to grasp.

Meanwhile, generative adversarial networks (GANs) produce stunningly real synthetic visual media. So do Diffusion Models. This is a bit technical – GANs employ an adversarial game between a generator and discriminator to produce realistic samples; Diffusion Models transform noise into data through an iterative diffusion process. Either way, it's becoming possible for our imaginations to become artefacts. Magic, again.

As today's techniques augment virtually every industry, AI appears to be steadily marching towards more flexible intelligence. Yet increased autonomy coupled with opaque inner workings raises concerns about potential harms. And biases lurking within data and algorithms require diligence. We stand at a pivotal crossroads in guiding these technologies towards benefitting humanity. What's quite tricky to concede is, AI is just mirroring us – there's good and bad, kindness and nastiness, benevolence and malevolence in the world. Remember, we were making AI be like us. Well, it is, in lots of ways.

It truly is a 'genie out of the bottle' moment in our lives. Now that AI is here, and undeniably present, how can we most benefit and least suffer from its position in our lives?

Glossary to Help Navigate Discussion Around AI

When you go to a 'foreign land' one of the things that can most undermine your confidence in participating in what's going on around you, is being unable to speak the local language. It's the same with AI. There's more 'foreign' vocabulary every month, as AI gathers pace and adoption. To help everyone not feel inadequate or anxious, I've organised AI into the key terms I've noticed.

It's ordered to follow the time-based narrative I've described in this chapter. It all makes sense. Gradually.

The advent of terms is arranged by decade, with a note on what the technical development was, followed by its broad consequence:

1950s–1960s

Artificial intelligence: Field aimed at creating machines capable of intelligent behaviour. AI has sought to reproduce facets of human cognition in machines. The goal of AI is to imbue machines with human-like intelligence to perform tasks that normally require human cognition.

Machine learning: AI techniques enabling systems to improve through data exposure without explicit programming. ML allowed more capable AI by learning from experience. Machine learning allows AI systems to learn and improve without needing humans to manually program every detail.

Artificial neural network: Computing system modelled on the brain's neuron connections that can learn from data. ANNs sparked new approaches to pattern recognition and classification. Neural networks enable computer systems to learn like the human brain by finding patterns in data.

1970s–1980s

Expert system: AI systems aiming to emulate specialised human expertise within a domain. Expert systems sought to automate and expand access to specialised knowledge. Systems apply AI to specific domains, allowing computers to provide expert guidance.

Computational linguistics: Study of using computers to understand and manipulate natural language. CL research sought to apply computational techniques to analyse language. Computational linguistics explores how to process natural human language using computational methods.

Algorithmic complexity: Concept analysing computational resource needs for algorithms. Understanding complexity allows optimised, efficient programs. Analysing algorithmic complexity helps optimise programs for speed and resource usage.

Backpropagation: Method for calculating error gradients in neural networks. Backpropagation enabled training deep neural network architectures. It allows deep neural networks to be trained through error minimisation.

Natural language processing (NLP): Field focused on enabling computers to understand, interpret, and generate human languages. Key focus areas of NLP include semantics (meaning), sentiment, summarising, translation, and dialogue systems.

Semantics: Linguistic study of meaning within language. In NLP, semantic analysis extracts and represents the meaning of text rather than just syntax. This enables interpreting intent and nuance.

1990s–2000s

Support vector machine: Algorithm that analyses data for classification and pattern recognition. SVMs excel at finding decision boundaries in complex data. SVMs are very effective for visual pattern recognition and classification tasks.

Convolutional neural network: Neural networks well-suited for processing grid-like structured data such as images. CNNs drove progress in computer vision and image recognition. CNNs enabled breakthroughs in image classification by mimicking visual cortex structure.

Markov model: System modelling randomly changing sequences of possible events. Markov models analyse probabilistic state transitions. They're useful for predicting the likelihood of different outcomes unfolding over time.

Reinforcement learning: AI technique allowing agents to determine ideal behaviours through trial-and-error interactions. RL is key to learning without explicit supervision. It helps AI agents learn by repeating actions that lead to rewards through self-guided exploration.

Semantic similarity: Measuring the degree of semantic relationship between linguistic items based on their meaning. Determining semantic similarity allows identifying related concepts and contexts.

Semantic role labelling: NLP technique identifying semantic relationships between entities in text such as agents, objects, and causes. Useful for information extraction applications.

2010s–Present

Generative adversarial network: AI model architecture effective for synthesising new data. GANs enabled major advances in generating realistic media. GANs can create highly realistic synthetic data like artificial photos that are indistinguishable from real images.

Transformer: Neural network utilising attention mechanisms to understand relationships in data like text. Transformers significantly improved natural language processing. The transformer architecture greatly boosted AI abilities for processing and generating human-like text.

Few-shot learning: Machine learning techniques able to solve new problems with limited sample data. Few-shot learning seeks to replicate human-like learning of new concepts from just a few examples.

Federated learning: Approach to train models collaboratively without aggregating user data. Federated learning enables collaborative AI training without compromising user data privacy.

Multimodal learning: Combining multiple modes like text, images, and audio to inform AI systems. Multimodal learning allows AI to interpret diverse data like images, text, and speech together like humans.

Prompt programming: New technique for instructing large language models using natural language prompts. Prompts provide intuitive control over capable foundation models. Prompt programming enables users to intuitively guide powerful AI systems.

Computer vision: Field developing automated analysis and understanding of visual data like images and video. CV extracts information from imagery for AI. Computer vision focuses on enabling AI systems to 'see' and analyse visual inputs like images and video.

Knowledge graph: Framework representing entities and relationships in knowledge bases. Knowledge graphs efficiently organise interlinked facts. Knowledge graphs structure information about real-world entities and their connections which AI can reason with.

Metalearning: ML technique focused on learning new skills and judgment from previous experience. Metalearning aims to bootstrap learning and reduce training time.

Adversarial attack: Test data deliberately modified to fool machine learning models and expose blind spots or vulnerabilities. Adversarial techniques reveal model limitations. Adversarial attacks help surface cases where AI systems fail in unrealistic or dangerous ways.

Bayesian deep learning: Applying principles of Bayesian inference to deep learning models to quantify uncertainty. It aims to create more cautious, robust models. Produces AI models that better handle uncertainty like humans.

Capsule network: ML approach using capsules to represent attributes of an object and their relationships. Capsule networks aim to enable stronger visual understanding and generalisation in AI.

Contrastive learning: Having neural networks discern highly similar images helps find distinguishing features. Contrastive learning improves visual recognition by focusing AI on subtle perceptual differences.

Diffusion models: Generative modelling technique that iteratively refines random noise into realistic samples. Diffusion models can generate highly realistic synthetic images, audio, and video.

Vision transformer: Applying the transformer architecture to computer vision, modelling global relationships in images. ViTs achieve state-of-the-art image classification results.

GPU (Graphics processing unit): Hardware accelerating parallel computations like neural net training. GPUs enabled the deep learning revolution in AI by speeding up intensive computations.

Foundation model: Reusable base model trained on broad data for adapting to downstream tasks. Foundation models provide generalised world knowledge to enable capable reasoning.

Reinforcement learning through human feedback: People provide non-expert guidance to shape reinforcement learning systems. Human feedback makes RL more practical while maintaining autonomy.

Semantic segmentation: Process of linking each pixel in an image to a relevant concept or classification. Allows richer scene understanding.

3
Parallels Between the Innovations of Publishing and AI

Phew. Those two histories were a lot to take in. I hope you found them coherent and accessible enough. There's a ton that's been left out but I hope it was a sufficient account of two histories that initially seem unrelated, for you to feel you understand the two protagonists in this story.

Diplomats, politicians, and lots of other groups in life get together, to get to know each other. In addition to being half-Egyptian, I'm also half-Irish, brought up around the world, in a United Nations family; my father was a peripatetic epidemiologist. I remember being astonished listening to a conversation in Ireland once. People were discussing a 'mixed marriage'. Having grown up in Africa, Asia, and the Caribbean, the term meant, to me, a 'mixed race' marriage, or at least, a mixed nationality union. Nope. It was, gasp, a wedding of a Catholic and a Protestant.

Why do I tell this story? So often what we make of things depends on how we've been culturally prepared, and the context in which we examine and reflect upon information. Ireland has been pretty parochial in its time and this story of two different parishes joining in holy matrimony was a big deal. Yet someone more concerned with knowing if a union was being made, say, between a Muslim and a Buddhist, would find the Irish scenario a breathtaking triviality – we're talking about two shades of Christianity, aren't we?

My point here is, publishing and AI can seem unrelated, even antagonistic, before one gets into them. In this chapter, I want to see if we can draw together some parallels. A long-established industry meets a very new one (that nevertheless has ancient roots). Might it be possible to see them as diplomats, getting to know each other amicably, finding common ground and whilst recognising differences, agreeing to co-exist in a productive manner? There need be no friction, even if a few sensible rules could help everyone get along OK. I feel there has been quite a lot of sulphur in the area, and a little de-escalation would do no harm.

Publishing and AI have a lot of things that are conceptually similar. They should, really – both are fertile and magnificent manifestations of human brain power. Let's keep that in mind. These parallels become most apparent when examining specific innovations over time.

Just as Johannes Gutenberg's printing press enabled the mass production and widespread distribution of books in the mid-15th century, the accumulation of vast datasets in recent decades has fuelled the development of powerful general AI models. Both fundamentally transformed access to information. Gutenberg meets ChatGPT, both enabling volumes of accessible data never previously seen.

Whereas digital publishing innovations allowed near instantaneous delivery of ebook files around the world, AI APIs today provide on-demand access to machine learning capabilities. You don't need your own super-computer. The frictionless availability brought by both expands possibilities beyond previous conceptions.

E-readers made books searchable and interactive through features like note-taking and dictionaries. Similarly, AI algorithms can power interactive, personalised book recommendations and responsive voice assistants. Readers gain deeper engagement. Already, the two worlds can't really help but begin to intertwine.

Both publishing and AI rely heavily on access to data – publishers need stories and content from authors, while AI systems need training data to learn from. The more data they have access to, the more knowledgeable and capable they become.

Network effects are crucial for growth and impact in both fields. The value of a publisher or AI system increases exponentially as more users engage with their content and services.

Reputation and trust are essential currencies. Publishers and AI companies alike succeed when they reliably provide high-quality offerings that meet audience needs. Brand integrity matters greatly.

In the 1990s, online book retailers utilised collaborative filtering algorithms to analyse purchase patterns and suggest books to customers. This laid the groundwork for modern AI-driven recommendation engines. Data insights improve discovery. They're nowhere near as good yet in books as they are in, say, music with Spotify and in films with Netflix, but this journey has begun.

Wonderfully, books are the richest of all human manifestations of creative genius, given their length, nuance, and intricacy. AI loves a bit of depth. It works well with subtlety, shades and delicacy. The two are perfect bed-fellows. Psychological matching of people with books, based on a subtle and nuanced comprehension of their values, interests, and emotions, is perfectly achievable with AI's understanding of books. Publishers can sell more, authors can reach further and readers find more fulfilling books. All can benefit from this symbiosis.

Just as audiobooks presented published works in conversational form, AI voice assistants like Siri and Alexa allow two-way verbal interactions. The human voice builds connection. Both industries strive for connection and accessibility.

Open source libraries in AI, like TensorFlow, help democratise development, much as digital publishing has, in part, removed gatekeepers to authorship. When knowledge is freely shared, innovation often thrives. The same sorts of dynamics have been operating in both industries.

Publishers have historically targeted specific genres, such as fiction, to perceived market opportunities. This is not unlike how modern AI application areas are rapidly expanding to address emerging, particularised needs. Understanding needs and priorities is fundamental to success in a world with a surfeit of choices of solutions. When you really look after someone, they really feel good about you. Publishing has tried to do that for millennia, and AI has rocketed to the same conclusion.

The publishing industry evolved from artisan book-making to scalable industrial production. Similarly, machine learning innovations have enabled the training of AI models at massive scale. But craftsmanship endures in writing and editing and increasingly in their marketing. Equally, honing the way an AI gathers, analyses and serves solutions, takes great attention to detail and clarity of mind. We are seeing the birth of AI-brands now, too.

Consolidation into dominant players shapes both fields, but diverse perspectives remain vital, for creativity and to ensure we do not end up in a homogenous mess of mediocrity. Five 'big' publishers command a huge swathe of the general book market today, with hundreds of thousands of 'smaller', or more focused, players serving specific needs, for authors and readers. There are hundreds of AI models around with truly extraordinary capability. Thinking just of the 'consumer-facing' ones, the world came to 'see' just how breathtaking AI has quietly become, in being interactive and seemingly sentient. That happened with ChatGPT's arrival. Bard came along too. Then Claude. And today as I write, LLaMA 2 has been made available. Like publishers, they have different capabilities, areas of focus, specialism, and excellence. I'll describe those later.

In so many ways, then, publishing and AI can interweave themselves, both representing fabulous ambition of the human mind – one in expressing it, the other in emulating it, both resulting in enrichment and enlightenment of those with whom they interact.

4
Great Things AI
Can Do In Publishing

We've seen that publishing and AI conceptually intertwine, sharing some common characteristics. I want to focus on how we can mobilise AI as a positive force in publishing.

We should first look at some other industries in which AI has had a palpably positive effect as that helps us to see clearly how publishing can learn from the positive experiences of others.

Retail

Retailers have leveraged AI to tackle longstanding challenges around predicting and aligning supply with consumer demand. Unexpected product demand fluctuations plagued retail with either lost sales from stockouts or mounting costs from overstock. Machine learning forecasting algorithms take in granular data on past sales performance, customer segments, marketing campaigns, seasonality, and external factors to more accurately predict future demand.

These AI systems outperform human judgement. With improved demand forecasts, retailers optimise inventory planning and reduce waste.

For publishers, AI forecasting presents similar opportunities to help predict book sales based on backlist performance, author brand, pre-orders, marketing plans, and market trends. This enables smarter print runs that save publishers from missed sales or high disposal costs when print runs go unsold.

Healthcare

You've probably heard the anecdote that AI keeps passing medical exams. There are some things which AI is just fabulously good at doing.

In healthcare, AI is improving diagnostic accuracy and consistency compared to human practitioners. Medical imaging analysis using computer vision pattern recognition can now detect tumours and anomalies at superhuman performance levels. By revealing hard-to-spot visual signs beyond human perception, AI systems help doctors diagnose disease earlier and more accurately. It's a great example of using a machine-collaborator to improve human performance.

Machine learning models can also process patient risk factors, family histories, biomarkers, and symptoms to predict diagnoses and future health risks. This is transforming the science of epidemiology and preventive medicine to the benefit of humanity.

Similarly in publishing, AI analysis can perform broad manuscript assessment by learning patterns from past successful works. This enhances editorial consistency. To be clear, this does not replace editorial nuance nor finesse, which is entirely based on human sensibilities. What it does offer is to take some of the hard ground-work off the overloaded task-lists of editors.

Banking

AI is really good at looking for patterns and connecting precursors with outcomes. For instance, it can tell that if three people stand in a particular configuration outside a building they are more likely to rob the place. Amazing.

The banking industry also applies AI to automate lending decisions for improved speed, fairness, and accuracy. Manual loan approval processes often demonstrated biases and oversights due to human limitations. AI credit models incorporate diverse applicant data – from income, employment, assets, and credit history to education, public records, and browsing habits – to learn fair predictive patterns. By evaluating applicants based on thousands of datapoints beyond human capacity to analyse. AI approval algorithms have reduced bias by about a third. A lot of people are more fairly treated because of AI.

Publishing faces similar diversity and bias challenges that AI techniques could help overcome through data-driven, impartial analysis of manuscripts author opportunities, and customer reliability. Eliminating manual biases could support publishing goals by amplifying under-represented voices. In short, AI can help more authors to have more opportunity, based on merit which can't be a bad thing.

Customer Service

It might appear ironic that AI improves personal service. It does, though.

Customer service leverages conversational AI to improve enquiry response rates. Brands have often struggled to staff call centres adequately to handle high consumer demand, resulting in long wait times, lost callers, and frustrated customers. Frequently maligned chatbots now deploy natural language processing to comprehend questions and provide answers from knowledge bases for millions of customers simultaneously. Response automation has allowed lots of companies to resolve over 80% of routine enquiries without human agents.

With many businesses, we're long past those annoying, endless menus that you invariably become lost within, and instead we've got conversational AI helping to guide us to a positive outcome with remarkable efficiency.

For publishers, AI chatbots could similarly expand author and reader support capacity to improve the discoverability and accessibility of books globally. By and large for publishers (with some important exceptions) their direct-to-consumer revenues are trivial relative to the industry's annual earning. Nevertheless, can you imagine calling a publisher and talking to an AI, to navigate through its catalogue, with the AI sensitive to your predilections and capable of guiding you to books you're sure to enjoy? Serendipity in discovery is lovely, but certainty is more rewarding. I'm reminded of a typically fun yet sage poem by Ogden Nash: 'Candy is Dandy, but Liquor is Quicker'.

Entertainment

There's a lot of AI going on here.

Interactive media like video games faced challenges keeping users engaged with static content. AI content generation adds dynamism by customising media experiences to user actions. Algorithms program variation into game levels, characters, music, and storylines so that the content adapts uniquely to the player, increasing replayability. The hope is that you end up feeling that the machine has understood you.

In publishing, AI presents opportunities to make stories more interactive. Conversational AI and narrative generation algorithms could allow readers to steer plot directions or generate scene variations tailored to their interests. This technology promises to expand creativity beyond linear stories into more participatory fiction.

Sure, we can worry about whether this just becomes machines creating content willy-nilly, but it can be great fun to imagine what 'might have happened' and to try a few different scenarios out. We must admit our minds wander, thinking 'what if this had happened instead of that...' AI enables us to float around a few tributaries off the main, author-driven narrative, and perhaps even creates a community of alternative 'takes' on a story. This has the potential to extend the lifetime and value of the manuscript.

Let's now pay attention to book publishing. It seems to me that AI can be deployed with publishers, authors, and readers, each in their own particular ways.

Putting AI to Work for Publishers

Efficiency Gains

AI loves complexity and the task of repetitive simplification. Advanced neural networks enable automation of complex production workflows like typesetting and layout.

Repetitive Jobs Like Title Setup

Machines love rules. They love to know what's allowed and what's prohibited, where the guardrails sit and where there's open space. AI follows rules precisely without human fatigue or oversight. Robotic process automation using smart software agents can replicate the manual steps for title setup in publishing systems.

By codifying workflows, AI automates repetitive data entry and production tasks like adding title details to databases, often more than 10x faster than humans. Pretty well everywhere, AI will be freeing up human time from repetitive, robotic tasks, to enable higher-value work to be done with creativity and imagination.

Streamlining Royalty Payments

Where there's a lot of data, organised in complex and sometimes labyrinthine fashions, AI gets busy and never gets into a flap. Advanced optical character recognition, natural language processing, and automation bots can digitise royalty reports, extract essential data, calculate payment amounts, and process transfers at high volumes. AI greatly speeds up payment processing while minimising errors from manual re-keying. This reduces the imperative to have repetitive, rote-like checking in royalty accounting departments.

Optimising operations

Demand Forecasting

Where there's a lot of disparate data, all of which could point in one direction, or another, the ability to run multiple models of what is likely to happen, with each element being weighted by data-driven analysis, transforms how we can think about what will happen next. Humans don't have the intellectual capacity, time, and often don't have the patience either, to do endless calculations of 'what if?'

AI demand forecasting leverages advanced predictive modelling capabilities that provide far greater accuracy than past data analysis for inventory planning and print run optimisation. Neural networks synthesise datasets on sales history, consumer trends, title performance predictors, and external factors. It all makes for far more precision, to reduce waste and maximise sales. It preserves finger-nails and protects from furrowed brows, too.

Smart Warehousing

Similarly, AI can work out space and logistics really well. It optimises warehouse operations, predicting demand and adjusting storage space accordingly. We see reduced energy consumption, lower transportation costs, and less waste due to 'thoughtful' inventory management. It's like an indefatigable, OCD friend who just likes to organise everything.

Measuring Marketing Impact

This is one of commercial life's greatest enigmas. Many CEOs will tell you that the least reliable report they have is from their CMO. 'We spent £10m on that last year, what did it produce in sales?' results in 'well, it's not just about sales, it's about building up brand equity and trust and that pays off in the long term'. How long? How much? 'I suppose you want the same again this year!'

AI looks at multi-variate data to quantify the influence of different campaigns on sales. It loves complexity and to go racing around it all to find the real story. There really is no riposte to the truth that data-driven AI insight surpasses subjective human judgement. It doesn't bring prejudice, or past experience, or conviction in magic. It's unrelentingly analytical in a way that puts marketing's toes to the fire.

Sustainability Initiatives

One of publishing's problems is paper. It's not great, in the first place. What's worse is, pulping. Or burning. Environmental impact analysis AI can assess the environmental impact of various book publishing processes, providing insights into areas where improvements can be made. For example, AI might evaluate the carbon footprint of different paper types, printing methods, or shipping routes, helping publishers prioritise sustainability initiatives. The industry clearly needs to get better and having a smart companion that figures out how to reduce waste seems to be a completely un-lamentable addition to how we do business.

Paper Selection

Although it's not the direct role of publishers, AI can assist in the publishing process, for example in selecting environmentally friendly paper options, taking into account factors such as recycled content, acid-free materials, and Forest Stewardship Council (FSC)-certified (and the like) sources. This helps reduce the carbon footprint of paper production and supports responsible forestry practices. Sure, we could do this ourselves, but it's a lot of work and it changes all the time. AI can stay on top of it all and make the 'wisest' decisions every time, based on the then-available information.

Core Publishing Workflows

Legal Work

Rights issues bedevil the industry, with an anachronistic, arcane system governing its commercial life, based on historical boundaries that have long since been superseded by everyday life. AI enables logical reasoning about rights issues. It provides legally nuanced contract review capabilities, to make sense of the conundra that face most publishing lawyers.

Logical reasoning algorithms parse terms holistically to derive deeper meaning, while graph-based relationship extraction can uncover conceptual links that human reviewers would likely miss. This level of AI-driven comprehension and analysis represents a major advance for automating the previously manual process of rights management. Even in a mess, AI can tidy up.

Translation

Machine translation has been on its way for a long time now. Anyone who uses, say, Google Translate today, will find it inestimably superior to the state it was in even five years ago.

Neural machine translation models learn contextual and stylistic nuances that far exceed capabilities of past human translation and dictionary-based approaches. By training on massive bilingual datasets, neural nets analyse patterns and understand linguistic usage in context, and at scale.

This enables automated translation that is more fluid, accurate, and scalable than human translators could produce manually for individual works. Publishers can now localise titles into countless languages at speeds never before achievable.

It's no longer art, where we discuss interpretation versus translation. It's just a process that gets done, beautifully, and almost instantly. Or course, this is all true for straightforward translation. Literary novels and poetry, for instance, still have some way to go ... and this is because of a recurring ingredient that is especially concentrated in those things: human, creative genius.

Editing and Proofing

I'm fully aware that as I write this chapter, there will be fears for the redundancy of some human capabilities and skills. The editor's role is nowhere near redundant!

But, holistic analysis and revision capabilities of large language models enable sophisticated editing automation, far superior to earlier grammar checkers and style guides. Neural network approaches represent an advance in contextual understanding that allows AI to assist with editing in ways not possible with rules-based tools. The machines 'get it'. This facilitates streamlining of the editing process, at least taking away the 'drudge-work' and leaving sophisticated human editors to add value in the most important places.

Put positively the 'grunt work' can be done by the machines now and the 'fairy dust' becomes the main contribution of the editor, who can do far more of it and without the morale- and time-sapping drudge of mundane proofing.

Connecting with Consumers

Optimised Product Descriptions

Large language models, like the GPT-series and many others, enable automated generation of book descriptions with unprecedented quality. They can be trained to produce marketing copy, rather than editorial summary – quite different things.

This reduces reliance on human marketers to manually craft descriptions based on personal reading and intuition, enabling far greater volumes of work to be done. AI systems can create unique marketing copy tuned to the specific voice of a given work. Or they can be instructed to take certain things into account, like the psychological profile of a book, to better match it to the frame of mind of a particular audience. In any case, there's a whole world of 'better presented' literature to populate, beyond a book cover and a few reviews.

Recommendation Engines

Publishing is fixated on email marketing lists. And talking to the same communities over and over. Best seller lists. PR. Meanwhile, most of the rest of the world has moved on to far more sophisticated approaches to engaging people with content.

Books have the most beautiful, nuanced, multi-layered psychological profiles, emotion-scapes and oceans of interest areas. Not only is this a bountiful expression of human genius, it's manna from heaven for AI to get to work on. There is so much to do to bring the full spectrum of (largely hidden, largely in the back-list) human genius into the limelight, for new audiences to enjoy and celebrate. AI can liberate human creativity.

AI filtering algorithms can incorporate multi-dimensional user data to understand individual preferences and make highly relevant, personalised suggestions. They work faster and further than human curators who are constrained by their own, inevitably limited, perspectives. Spotify does this with music. Netflix, with flicks on the net. But books, with evidently so much greater depth than either of those artistic expressions, have so far languished with relatively restricted thinking. Like Science Fiction? Here's another dozen sci-fi books for you. It's really time for this game to be upped.

Publishing is lagging behind music and movies in adopting AI opportunities. It can close the gap quickly and present itself in a much more contemporary and dynamic fashion.

Putting AI to Work for Authors

There are many ways in which having a powerful companion and collaborator can make life easier. AI can enable authors to focus upon only what excites and motivates them. There are also some ways in which AI threatens authors.

Automating Research

It can take forever to master a subject, or to know with authority how something works, or to be able to describe in intimate details an act of espionage or sexuality. It might be fun and instructive to do all that, but it takes time and, usually, money and connections.

I'm aware that many authors enjoy the process of research. While you look at things, your mind is creatively assembling a narrative or an insight or a piece of dialogue. And it can be fun and spiritually rewarding to travel and explore things about which you wish to write.

All the same, AI is like the smartest, fastest, most encyclopaedic friend you've ever had. If I want to know how the FBI works in Virginia, or how to harvest rubber sap from a tree outside Kuala Lumpur, or who invented the vibrator and why, I can fill my mind with ten different perspectives on all that, in seconds. Sure, it begins to need different skills in gathering, processing and outputting knowledge, but it leaves an awful lot more time for creativity and origination of thought and content. AI can bring out the best in humans.

Semantic search algorithms and natural language processing enable automation of research at a scale far beyond human capabilities. It quickly supersedes our past reliance on manual literature reviews and basic keyword-based search engines. AI techniques rapidly analyse millions of sources, uncovering contextual information and pertinent facts that exceed what authors could access through individual human effort or now historical search-engines. This exponential augmentation of knowledge acquisition and extraction is a game-changer for authors. We're all on mind-bending substances now.

Augmenting Creativity

I think we have to see AI like a calligrapher's brush. If I ask you to see 'calligraphy', most of you just conjured up Japanese script, in black ink, drawn with a large brush, and if you thought about it, the bristles might have been a squirrel's or a badger's – something exotic anyway. It's a long chain of 'technology-enhanced production'.

Most creativity uses tools. Musicians use guitars and reverb buttons and production software that bends and tunes the human-produced sounds we accept as art. Sculptors spin clay. Seamstresses plunge needles back and forth in strings of textiles. Architects use physics to figure out how a cantilevered façade can give the illusion of a great mass, floating.

AI Helps Authors to Write.

Creative text generation models – and there are genuinely more, new ones each week – allow computers to provide writing inspiration tailored to an author's style and genre. It sits alongside human imagination and basic computerised idea generators. By learning from example prompts, AI can output plot concepts, character details, and settings that match an author's voice and creative vision.

Is this so different from sitting in a bar and chatting to a friend about an idea? I know it's a lot less 'human' – or analogue – and none of us want the bar, the chat or the drink to drain away, but what we seek is affirmation of ideas, or sometimes dismissal or iteration of them. We do this in an accidental fashion in today's life – AI is making it reliable, instantly available, immediately productive. AI supplements human ideation.

Drafting Assistance

Being really crude about it, we write a lot of repetitive stuff. Sometimes we are unbelievably creative. The former is grist to the AI mill, the latter far beyond it because it's unpredictable. It's as simple as that. AI predicts. Humans make random stuff up.

Large language models can produce draft text that goes beyond outline placeholders by learning high-level structure and patterns from example works in specific genres. This provides authors with more developed early drafts to iterate on rather than starting from scratch. Pretrained language models are able to generate multi-paragraph draft text that has coherency and conforms to genre conventions. We don't need to start from blank pages.

Unless we're thinking of the next *War and Peace*, or Ian McEwan's *Concrete Garden*, AI can quickly assemble an acceptable draft of a discussion of tidal flow on the Thames or why particular road furniture is associated with lower accident rates – for us to add flourish and poise and signature semantic structures.

AI-Powered Editing

We all need to proof (generally it's only the most fastidious amongst us who love that phase of writing) and we often need discipline we won't bring to our own extravagances and flights of linguistic fancy. AI intervenes, when we call it to do so, in a non-judgmental, entirely servile fashion, proffering sensible suggestions for parsimony of language and accuracy of language, here and there. It's about the easiest criticism there has ever been to take.

AI techniques like neural network revision models and attention mechanisms work by understanding text holistically. It allows AI editing assistants to make meaningful suggestions tailored to the broader context rather than just fixing minor errors. Attention mechanisms allow AI models to analyse how each word relates to the overall meaning and flow rather than just checking isolated sentences. It's pretty vanilla stuff that it does but we all wash vegetables and that's really what AI does to our scripts – it just suggests, with no fuss at all, how we can improve it.

Interactive Storytelling

The conjunction of writing with 'gaming' will no doubt happen more frequently. Already we are seeing cartoon franchises become films and toy franchises also morph into movies. Content is shape-shifting as commercial agendas to exploit original creativity into every expressible format achievable becomes endemic.

So, authors can do the same with their creations, too. AI can collaborate endlessly with a reader who wants to create their own ending to a formerly mono-thematic story.

AI collaborative storytelling allows interactive fiction with adaptable plots that respond uniquely to the reader, representing a new frontier not possible with static, pre-set stories. We can't do this on the printed page, but we can do it pretty well in every other medium that expresses the story.

This expands creative possibilities for authors by enabling participatory worlds that can be dynamically shaped by readers' actions. Whereas past stories followed predefined arcs, AI can enable customisable narratives that reinvent themselves in real-time based on user input. This provides nearly limitless opportunity for emergent storytelling.

The author is the font. AI helps the splashing.

Streamlining Manuscript Preparation

Should it be double-spaced? Presented in a specific combination of fonts and sizes?

Intelligent automation of formatting and manuscript preparation saves authors effort over past manual work that strictly just followed style guides. This streamlines getting a manuscript ready for submission, freeing up authors to spend time on more substantive creative tasks.

Advanced AI algorithms can accurately handle rote formatting tasks based on analysis of publishers' specifications, exceeding the capabilities of find-and-replace or simple scripting. Does anyone really love conformative admin?

AI frees the author from the patience-sapping job of getting manuscripts ready for someone else's procedural purposes. Tell it what you need and it'll do it in a flash for you.

Analysing Writing Patterns

We all write in a way that we believe will successfully involve the reader, and be authentic to our authorial voice. This usually involves quite idiosyncratic patterns of grammar, vocabulary and structure.

AI detects subtle linguistic patterns and stylistic trends in a writer's work that would be difficult to identify manually. By examining factors like vocabulary, sentence structure, and pacing at scale across an entire corpus, AI gives authors data to help improve their craft in ways not possible through human close reading.

All this empowers authors with concrete and often subtle insights into their own writing tendencies. It would tell me that I love an ellipsis ... so much so that I use it as often as I can ... and that can be quite jarring to the non-ellipsis-loving reader ... *tant pis*!

Putting AI to Work for Readers

Personalised Recommendations

As previously mentioned in slightly different terms, we've become very accustomed to being 'suggested' what we would like. We adopted a sort of 'knowing passivity' – bring me what you know I like and maybe I'll give you my time.

Netflix and Spotify have become past-masters at this, but it's present in wider recommendations to us, too – like hotels we'd like, places we'd like to eat, whether we should buy a cauldron if we're into witchery, and even who might be our most enduring or exciting romantic partner.

But books? Bestseller lists and past purchase behaviour. It needs to move on. The only way you'll get what you like is being active, beyond what you need to do in nearly every other walk of life. Readers live in a world characterised by anachronistic suppliers of content. That's not sustainable.

By analysing factors like purchase history, ratings, reviews, and browsing habits, AI can suggest relevant niche titles that human curators lacking this holistic view may have overlooked. This enables a level of personalisation not achievable through human recommendation alone.

More sophisticated approaches will hove into view very soon, including understanding a person's psychological stance in the world – which values they espouse, what is emotive to them, which areas of interest are most animating – and AI will be able to match readers with books with unprecedented likelihood of being fulfilling. And this is because books are uniquely deep on population by these things – each work is a vast repository of human insight, ready to be mined, brought to the surface and burnished, to shimmer in the reader's eye.

Increasing Accessibility

There are books that we will always want read to us by the author, or a 'famous actor'. But there's also a huge amount of content which is more pedestrian than that, which people might need to consume in far more accessible ways.

Automated narration, powered by text-to-speech, expands access for print-impaired readers far beyond the fixed inventory constraints of human-narrated audiobooks. AI narration makes exponentially more written content available in audio format than the limited recording capacity of studios and voice actors.

It's also true that we are generally barred from enjoying many great works of human ingenuity simply because we can't understand the languages in which they're written (and they might not previously have been commercially viable to have translated, printed, bound, exported, distributed, and retailed).

Automated multilingual translation expands access to literature from around the world for readers of any language. Neural machine translation models fluently translate books into countless languages, overcoming human translator scarcity. This enables cross-cultural literary exploration at unprecedented scale.

I was lucky to find *Momotaro, the Peach Boy* and read it to my children in English. I bet there are countless other Japanese gems of literature which might have ignited their imaginations, if I had been able to find and read them in English. Gradually, the cellular structure of the human hive will be simplified by AI, so we are no longer cut-off from other cultures by the simple matter of how it expresses itself in language. AI can be culturally transformative, bringing previously separated peoples together. Have you ever thought you might like to read a Mongolian thriller now that you've exhausted Skandi-noire? With AI, there's nowhere you can't go.

5
Things to Fear with AI

Not many of us are comfortable when the status quo is interrupted. We tend to crave the steady, the known, the system we've learned to work. Change brings rupture, often realigns hierarchies; people who were essential can seem less so, ones who were peripheral become central. Innovation catalyses many of these realignments in our working lives.

New technologies very often spark apprehension and distrust when first introduced before eventually becoming widely adopted. Looking at examples from the past few decades provides perspective on how early fears around transformative innovations eventually subside as benefits become apparent and familiarity grows. We do get used to change. Often, we make the initial expression of an innovation better, through resistance then iteration, and finally by assimilation.

The **internet** initially sparked fears around, and gained notoriety for, enabling cybercrime and piracy. People were afraid of predators, hackers, and privacy violations caused scepticism.

However, its convenience and access to information won over the public. To think we once had deliveries of enormous, printed Yellow Pages! The internet's communication and commerce capabilities are now indispensable (despite its remaining risks and the abuses we see within it).

Mobile phones produced fears about distracted driving and etiquette when first popularised. They were well-founded and the industry and law-makers ensured that such behaviours were quickly curtailed. Early studies sparked health concerns over radiation exposure from handsets. While risks remain, mobile phones are now ubiquitous communication tools, inextricable from modern life. (Re)-imagine how we lived before we could text, and consider how many of us today ever use a 'land-line'.

Digital photography and editing prompted concerns about manipulation, misinformation, and the end of photojournalism. While valid in some cases, the public overwhelmingly embraced the instant gratification and creative possibilities. Digital images are now the norm. The idea of going to a store with your roll of negatives and returning days later to see your prints seems ante-diluvian.

Social media were decried for encouraging narcissism, decreasing attention spans, and spreading misinformation. But the desire for connection and community prevailed. Responsible information sharing remains a concern, but social media are entrenched, credited for advancing causes and creating thriving communities, of almost every colour and hue. It's quite likely that social media have even decreased the use of sleeping pills, as people lull themselves to sleep with their ever-emissive screens.

Cloud computing encountered hostility, with concerns expressed about privacy, security, and reliability of remote data storage. But the benefits of conveniences like streamed media and anytime access to information were irresistible. The cloud is now fundamental despite its known vulnerabilities. We synch things all day long, with hardly a care or concern.

Initial negativity towards new technologies is understandable and probably inevitable. The value that AI promises for transforming publishing should be weighed in light of how past innovations gained acceptance. With responsible development and well-judged implementation, AI can, like other technologies before it, follow the path from doubtful novelty to beneficial advancement. It's a familiar journey: remember the Sumerian clay-tablets being superseded by Egyptian papyrus, before Gutenberg, Claxton, and others paved the way for ebooks to permeate our lives. We've accommodated great change many times before.

Let's explore how AI might challenge and cause concern to publishers, authors and readers.

Risks for Publishers

Publishers face a number of risks related to emerging AI technologies. While not exhaustive, these risks centre around issues of legal uncertainty, business model disruption, workforce impacts, algorithmic bias, and marketing measurement challenges.

Legal and Rights Issues with AI-Generated, Written Content

The legal status of AI-generated works remains unclear, causing publishers uncertainty about intellectual property rights. At the time of writing in August 2023, there have been several law-suits against AI companies, complaining about copyright infringement. Judges have generally concluded that though the training sets used for Large Language Models have ingested copyrighted works, they do not materially harm those works and therefore their continued use is legal.

Training algorithms on copyrighted data also raises questions around derivative works and fair use exemptions. Until AI content has clear copyright protections, publishers risk litigation by claiming ownership of essentially authorless pieces. It's clear that publishers rightly wish to honour and protect authors' works and their own assets, but it is not yet obvious that simply by reading and learning the content of those works, 'an AI' then specifically uses that piece of work for gain. There will be continuing challenges around copyright for some, not least because of the existential nature of copyright to the commercial stability of publishing (and other media) companies.

Loss of Control Over Distribution Channels and Discovery

Although there is not much 'direct-to-consumer' business, publishers may lose direct relationships as AI systems intermediate book discovery and delivery. Algorithms can analyse individual interests and recommend books without brand loyalty. Unlike human curators, AI platforms owe and show no allegiance, potentially commoditising books into interchangeable products. This disintermediation threatens publishers' agency in guiding readers. (On the other hand, AI also offers the opportunity for a real growth in D2C revenues.)

Pressure on Business Models

Widespread AI-generated content could drastically lower production costs and disrupt traditional publishing models. Advanced natural language models can rapidly produce book-length manuscripts for little expense. As creation costs fall, publishers may struggle to support overhead previously associated with high-cost creative content. Automation of the full publishing workflow could pressure margins and viability. There is likely to be much more self-publishing and that content is likely to be of a much higher quality, augmented by AI, challenging the pre-eminence of a publishing house in the journey of an author's work.

Job Losses in Production

Production automation could displace human roles in editing, typesetting, design, and printing. As AI handles rote tasks, jobs requiring pattern recognition over discretion may be eliminated. While new roles could emerge, workforce disruption is likely as machines gain capabilities once requiring specialised skills. Without wishing to be anything other than factual, this is a pattern as a consequence of every technological innovation over time. Usually, this change in application of labour produces new roles and opportunities, often with higher value human contributions.

Backlash Over Perceived Greed, In Replacing Staff with Algorithms

It's fair to fear that there will be a lack of human curation in AI-driven recommendation engines. Currently, there is an abundance of such human judgment in book publishing, remarkably more so than in competitive-for-attention fields, like movies and music. Purely data-driven AI recommender systems will initially ignore subjective dimensions of editorial curation and bookseller relationships. Removing humans from the loop therefore loses their judgment, category knowledge, and qualitative factors. It is, however, quite likely that AI systems will learn to be nuanced and subtle, and to work out far more than simple book structure, instead increasingly understanding the human values that editors currently identify and prioritise.

Over-Reliance on Purchase Correlations

There is real difficulty in tracking returns on investment of AI marketing tools versus traditional channels. The often opaque inner workings of machine learning advertising algorithms make it hard to understand their decision-making. Isolating the return on investment of AI marketing from organic discovery and promotions is therefore challenging. With online attribution models in flux, publishers may be unsure where to allocate resources between new AI tools versus tried channels. This obviously carries the risk of misjudging impact. It's likely that there will be new snake-oil salespeople abounding as this all settles into place.

Risk of Perpetuating Biases If Training Data Is Limited

Biases and limitations in data used to train AI inevitably propagate through machine learning models. They can get stuck and sometimes that's in an unpleasant rut. Algorithms can amplify prejudices and disproportionately impact marginalised groups. Creating inclusive, representative datasets requires conscientious effort. Publishers need to safeguard against unfair biases emerging in automated publishing processes – doing so will necessitate hiring and training AI-sophisticated staff on the Publisher side of this equation.

Authors

Deliberately, this section seeks to identify where there should be proper alarm about AI.

Authors face profound disruptions from industrialised AI-generated content that could undermine livelihoods and devalue creative craft.

The sheer endless volume of algorithmic books threatens to saturate the market, condition readers to accept diluted quality, and render human writers unable to compete economically.

Plagiarism of unique authorial voices also raises originality concerns.

Even setting aside economic impacts, creative integrity is challenged by the notion of literature produced devoid of authentic human connection to resonate with audiences.

Additional risks arise from potential inaccuracies and lack of nuance when relying on AI for research assistance.

Authors need AI that uplifts, not supplants, their irreplaceable creativity.

AI-generated Content Devaluing Creativity and 'Flooding' the Market

A deluge of AI-authored books risks saturating the market (even beyond ISBN inflation), devaluing writing craft, and conditioning readers to accept subpar quality worries many. Some see creative expression as under attack by data-driven algorithms churning out endless content. Even if mostly used for templated genres, the scale of AI generation could degrade perceptions of artistic merit. As such work is essentially free of cost and can arrive in enormous volume, there is a risk that the uninitiated reader will find themselves mired in anodyne content, ultimately risking that the reader may suffer the Shakespearian woe of 'surfeiting, the appetite may sicken and so die'.

Plagiarism of Unique Authorial Styles by AI Imitators

AI language models can rapidly absorb and mimic individual authorial styles. Training on an author's previous works risks AI regurgitating highly-derivative imitations of original creative voices. Even training a model on multiple diverse writers can produce an unintentional pastiche infringing on authorial rights. This potential plagiarism threatens creative integrity. It is certainly a risk that well-trained AI can sound an awful like someone we know. Even now, one can train it to produce content 'in the style of...' and this could run amok.

Tireless AI Content Creators with Lower Costs

AI poses an existential threat to human authors' competitiveness by infinitely scaling output at negligible cost. They just don't get tired. And if well-instructed, there is almost no volume that they would baulk at producing. No writer can keep pace with algorithms that neither tire nor require income. Authors fear being unable to monetise their skills and disappearing into irrelevance as AI overwhelmingly floods publishing.

Lack of Human Appreciation for AI-generated Works

Creative gratification stems from connecting with readers, and this is currently largely impossible for AI that lacks lived experience. Machine learning cannot yet exhibit much empathy, or truly grasp emotional impacts on readers. Even if reaching technical parity with human writing, AI may fail to elicit profound appreciation for the fruits of its own expression.

There is, however, a notion of 'emergence' in the AI world – where the creators of the models cannot understand how the machines do things they truly were not trained to manifest. It's still unsure, but there is a real likelihood that AI will gradually display independent character, and with that, personality, and consequently, to be able to form relationships. In this scenario, apart from everything else, it's likely AI will indeed be able to produce manuscripts that exhibit many more of the qualities that currently allow us to discriminate between machine and human-authored works.

Loss of Income if AI Reduces Compensation

If publishers and/or readers shift to utilising predominantly cheap AI content, author compensation models could collapse. Confronting an endless supply of inexpensive AI books, publishers may slash advances and royalties. This severe income loss, before human creativity is matched, could devastate authors financially, widening inequality.

Risk of Bias, Errors, and Misrepresentation In AI Research Tools

Flaws and biases in AI-generated research sources could propagate misinformation or improperly portray subjects. Models trained only on narrow world views risk representing cultures, identities, and histories unethically. Relying on algorithms that are lacking in appropriate context could contort perspectives, even inadvertently. Authors who trade in the distant, exotic research trip, for the immediacy and convenience of a desk-based, AI-powered 'virtual' immersion in a subject, do risk having an unguarded, unverified deep-dive into a highly distorted representation of that which they wish to interrogate.

Readers

Over-Personalisation Limiting Exposure to New Ideas

While AI personalisation provides a tailored reading experience, it risks creating cocoons devoid of challenging viewpoints. Hyper-specific customisation by algorithms seeking to appease tastes and beliefs may isolate readers from unfamiliar ideas. This intellectual 'bubble' effect could entrench biases and eliminate enriching surprise from diverse art. In short, there's a risk that you get what you like. And we know that variety is the spice of life, so this is not a great future for readers.

Filter Bubbles and Lack of Transparency In AI Recommendations

It's hard to figure out how proprietary AI systems determine their recommendation systems. What they might do, though, is cause readers to be sequestered in algorithmic bubbles shaped by previous behaviours without realising they are subject to hidden biases. Readers might struggle to keep control of their intellectual learning journeys and general reading experiences.

Risk of Manipulation by Hyper-Targeted AI Marketing

Granular reader profiling by AI could enable manipulation for marketing purposes. Models discerning vulnerabilities may exploit them through psychological nudges designed to maximise consumption. While influencing choice is intrinsic to advertising, finely tuned AI targeting poses risks of 'over-reach'.

Loss of Serendipity and Curation In Discovery

AI-guided discovery risks losing the unexpected delights of browsing and curation. While improving targeting, algorithms lack human appreciation of intrinsic book value beyond measured popularity. The serendipity of discovering an overlooked gem recommended by a discerning seller may disappear into cold, statistically-driven automation. 'Stumbling upon' a great read becomes ever less likely, unless the reader deliberately maintains a habit of being in the analogue world of bookshops.

Concerns About Surveillance Based on Reading Behaviour

AI is good at surveying, or let's call it surveillance of reading choices, and this could be especially important around sensitive material. Profiling reading habits and preferences is valuable for personalisation but could be abused for social manipulation or control if not protected.

Limitations in Understanding Context of AI-Generated Content

Understanding narrative context is challenging when engaging with AI-authored works lacking singular creative vision or deliberate crafting of interwoven themes. Even if reaching technical parity, AI-generated books inherently lack the intentionally layered narrative resonance of human imaginations. Put bluntly, the reader becomes subjected to monotonous, monothematic works, lacking in creative surprise and unexpected 'twists'.

Subtleties of Life Elude AI

Human creative works, at their best, inspire profound emotions and mental stimulation. One can feel profoundly moved by them. But AI lacks life experiences to infuse personal connections to art. This can make them pretty anodyne. Algorithms can't, yet, channel raw feeling. So reading too much AI-authored work can deaden the sensibilities of human nature. It's like eating too much carbohydrate with not enough protein.

Overreliance on Convenience Over Focused Engagement

The frictionless convenience of AI recommendations provides instant gratification but discourages the attentive mindset needed for engaging literature. Society's increasing expectation of ease risks impairing capacities for serious reading. Prioritising personalised convenience over appreciating creativity could diminish literature's cultural role. This plumbs fairly deeply into a wider question about the role of literature, and information, in today's society and learning culture.

Summing up

AI is certainly here to stay, and like with so many of its forerunners, humanity will interact with it, evolve it, make it acceptable, and finally assimilate it.

The publishing industry is understandably apprehensive about AI given the disruptive changes it may bring and risks involved. However, we can take encouragement from how societies eventually adapted to beneficial new technologies in the past once drawbacks were addressed. Through responsible development and prudent regulation, AI's positives for publishing can hopefully outweigh the negatives.

For publishers, maintaining transparency around AI usage while safeguarding against bias and job loss will be critical. Developing representative datasets, testing models rigorously, and keeping humans involved in key decisions can help reduce risks. Publishers will need to communicate frequently with creators and readers to understand AI concerns across the industry. There will need to be much more integration of publishers, authors, and readers in various forums.

Authors justifiably worry about the economic and creative threats posed if AI text generation comes to dominate publishing. However, human imagination seems unlikely to be surpassed entirely. Indeed, AI nudges humans even more fully to embrace its unique unpredictability, originality and sheer randomness of creative thought. There are also opportunities to employ AI as a collaborative tool for research, ideation, and efficiency.

Readers benefit from transparency from publishers and booksellers about how AI shapes recommendations to avoid over-personalisation. Alternatives retaining human curation can ensure that our uniquely 'random' ways of thinking remain pedestalised and valued.

Through ethics policies, diversity initiatives, responsible implementation of capabilities, and fairness to human collaborators, the publishing industry can hopefully steer AI's course to augment creativity rather than undermine it.

The rich history of publishing has constantly shown its resilience and propensity for adaptation to disruptive innovations. Though challenges await, AI will hopefully inspire authors and delight readers as much as it unsettles the status quo. If wisely managed, AI will have net positive impacts, just as past technologies evolved from feared disruptions into indispensable aids.

6
Does AI Change the
Place of Literature in Society?

We might be at an inflection point in society, even civilisation.

Humans are broadly composed of implicit and explicit systems. We feel, and we think. One is largely instinctive, the other highly considered. It's a repetitive theme in life... 'I should have known better', 'I knew it was wrong but I still did it', 'all the evidence was I shouldn't do it, but I went ahead anyway, and I was right to!', 'he had this amazing reputation, but the moment I shook hands with him I knew I'd never like him', 'I can't put my finger on why I know there's a great opportunity here, but I know there is...'. There is a running tug-of-war in our lives between what we feel we should do and what we think we should do.

In different environments, we tend to favour one over the other. In business, our explicit system that favours rational, slow thinking – commonly referred to by neuroscientists as System 2 – tends to win. In love, our implicit system that favours emotional, faster decision-making tends to drive us, commonly referred to as System 1.

What's the relevance? AI is really good at System 2, explicit thinking. It can gather and organise, parse and consider, and deliberate with immense rationality. More and more, society is likely to leave System 2, explicit, largely rational thinking, to AI. It'll make sensible, safe, well-weighted decisions. Tesla is iterating this with every mile its cars travel. They make fewer and fewer mistakes, already having surpassed a human's ability to make sound judgments when in control of a vehicle. MRI scans are better evaluated by AI, which takes billions of similar images into account, in the blink of a human eye, never fatiguing, never misjudging because of distraction or mood.

Humans, then, will increasingly be the source of system 1, Implicit, emotionally-biased, creative 'content' in the world. So often that is expressed in literature. Despite the millennia of technological innovation and change in writing, sharing, publishing, literature basically embodies the unique human ability to FEEL.

How does this matter? AI will increasingly be granted permission to make our mundane, 'sensible' decisions. Traffic management. Aircraft control. Warehousing efficiency. Payment schedules. Food transport. Medical intervention. It'll be everywhere, making us safer and better ordered.

Meanwhile, AI trains. It is hungry to learn. It needs reward models that teach it how to weigh decisions, to know when actions it recommends result in good outcomes, and when they don't. The old adage of garbage in, garbage out persists in a world increasingly ordered by AI. So it is incumbent on us, the feelers, the emoters, the empaths, the gut-instincters, to hold up our end, and express ourselves, to train AI to our purposes and with our ethical standards passionately expressed. We must write. For now, literature is the most precious training set most models learn from. AI will understand that humans are not always rational, not always sensible, not always predictable. There is much fear that AI will take over the world but the fundamental truth is that we are impossible to emulate – and we must continue to be expressive of our uniquely human powers of creating something out of nothing.

Gradually, there will be a division of labour, between humans and that which we deliberately sought to introduce as our companion in the world – artificial intelligence. We will increasingly stream information, assembling it, processing it, and making decisions from it, serviced by AI. And we'll need to learn to trust our instincts, to listen to our inner voices, to follow our feelings. This will be a not frictionless union for a while, as we learn how to give new proportion to each, in different circumstances and environments. But AI-assisted life is here to stay.

Let's consider some of the changes we're witnessing.

Throughout human history, the veneration of knowledgeable individuals, those encyclopaedic repositories of information, has been the norm. We have long held the belief that the possession of vast knowledge and the ability to recall it effortlessly are the hallmarks of intellect and wisdom.

'Being brainy' has been awesome and is normally identified by knowing tons of things. Lawyers refer to 'my learned friend', explicitly honouring their colleagues with recognition of the scale of their bank of knowledge.

We now stand at a point where the emphasis is shifting from mere accumulation of knowledge to the art of gathering, processing, and making informed decisions from information in real-time. Of course, we have not been dumb receptacles for information – Newton did a lot of thinking to figure out gravity, he didn't just watch the apples falling.

This paradigm shift, which I abbreviate as 'moving from hard-disking to streaming', heralds the dawn of a new age of wisdom.

For as long has been recorded, societies have celebrated and esteemed scholars. These erudite individuals, amazing keepers of knowledge, were considered the elite, the guiding lights who shaped the path of progress. From ancient sages to Renaissance polymaths, the reverence bestowed upon them was unparalleled. Their intellectual prowess commanded respect and admiration. Professors were the supercomputers of their age. They had the biggest hard disks.

As we venture further into the digital age, and especially now, the era of AI, we find ourselves standing at the edge of a profound transformation. The exponential growth of technology, and the unfathomable wealth of information available at our fingertips, have paved the way for a new form of wisdom.

AI's ability to give immediate access to information, but also to find, then present original perspectives on it, is stunning. It's hard to habituate to its uncanny ability to assemble, organise, and distil meaning from content.

Those who will now succeed in all aspects of life will understand how to ride the growing tsunami of immediately available multiple-perspectives, making sense of them, and leveraging the power of immediacy and multiplicity to make informed decisions. The best outcome is to harness AI's ability to present data-driven recommendations and for us to allow our feelings to filter it further, trusting our human instinct. Of course, if Tesla's AI stops the car at a busy intersection, we should not 'feel' we could 'wriggle through'. We will, however, 'know' that despite it being 'safe' to sit in a lightless room for 48 hours, it is not good for our mental health.

In this new era of permanent connectivity and constant data influx, wisdom manifests itself as the capacity to sift through an abundance of information, discerning relevance from noise, and critically analysing its implications. This includes sensing our way through AI-driven suggestions.

It may not seem so, but when you ask an 18-year-old which movie would be best to watch, they immediately and adroitly sift through multiple streams of availability, pricing, reviews, and cultural impact, to arrive at a swift recommendation. They're parsing and concluding in real time.

Word of mouth and singular points of review don't seem at all reliable to them. Their personally curated ability to gather, process, and decide within multiple streams of information supersedes the traditional manual process, making decision-making swifter and more circumspect.

The presence of algorithms from Spotify, Netflix, Snapchat, TikTok and others, is daily supplanting traditional news and information channels with their singular editorial perspectives. Those things that have seemed trivial distractions, that have worried parents with concerns of making our children into ADHD, micro-attenders, have actually been tuning a new generation of information-hungry, sophisticated processing units.

Wisdom, in our new AI age, is about embracing complexity and uncertainty, acknowledging that true understanding lies not in the storage and recall of facts, but in the ability to contextualise and apply them effectively, in real time. To do so, we use our own system 2 rationality, augmented by AI, plus our unique system 1 instinct.

Critical thinking, analytical skills, and the ability to discern credible information from misinformation will need to be at the core of our educational systems. We need society to have a generalised expertise in understanding of 'signals' and to be able to judge the truth from the interpolations arising from them. We must understand how AI gets to where it does, and be able to accept or contradict it.

Wisdom, in this new world, will accelerate, be democratised, and lead to a great refinement in the conduct of our lives. Conflicts will be more amicably settled, as evidence will show it to be the most productive solution to disagreements. Creativity will flourish, as it is shown that the greatest advances flow from unleashing the human mind from doubt and enabling it to conceive with freedom and abandon.

What's most exciting is that our new leaders will be employing machines and their data, to release human genius in a way never before seen, to create, to invent, to imagine, in a care-free fashion. 'The freedom of a tight brief' is what we can look forward to – with much less casting around in the darkness, and far more certainty of positive outcomes in the light.

Machines are freeing humans to be more, human.

Write, Write, and Write More!

What of 'literature'? It becomes ever more important. It is the implicit, to balance what will swiftly be a preponderance of explicit. Human feeling will be the ying, to AI's thinking yang.

This might have all sorts of effects. It's not difficult to imagine (an AI would predict) a world where science becomes largely what machines do, and art is the preserve of humans, who dream, create, and inspire, pursuing random and illogical flows of feelings (and thoughts), assembling them into narratives that they communicate to others. Mostly through literature.

The world that balances human intelligence with artificial intelligence needs us to continue exhibiting magical, human originality of thought, displaying whimsy, fancy and fantasy, and sometimes expressing instinct and primal sense ... all these things become the superior backbone of any body of knowledge or, in our new parlance, 'the training set'. To continue the theme, human intelligence will largely be system 1, implicit and emotional, and Artificial Intelligence will largely be system 2, explicit and rational.

If we want our AI to be helpful and reliable collaborators as we navigate the future, if we want them to be circumspect and cautious in their offers of conclusions and perspectives, if we want them to weigh and balance, then it's an imperative that we re-double our efforts to fill them with thoughtful, creative, considered, funny, brilliant expositions of humanity. They must understand that there are qualities quite beyond them, which are justifiably taken into account. AI is what we teach it to be.

All that we wish to preserve and by which we wish to be characterised, we must produce more and more of. Never has there been a greater need for humans to express themselves in the written word.

7
Make Friends with the New (AI) Kids on the Block

In practical terms, publishers, authors, and readers are likely to use the 'chat' iterations of AI that are arriving in our midst. There are legions of 'hot-takes' on how to use them, with reams of 'prompt tips' appearing everywhere from LinkedIn to TikTok and journals, newspapers, and TV shows. As a general comment, we are learning that we can ask the AI to write 'as if you are a critic, a chief executive, a novice', or whatever and it will oblige, taking that perspective on whatever your subject matter is. In short, role-playing and clear direction as to what is needed, is the best way to begin to great value out of your interactions. More granular advice abounds everywhere on the internet.

As these will be our new companions at work and play, this chapter introduces the four main protagonists that exist as I write this.

First, let's refamiliarise ourselves with two generations of 'tech brands' that have become part of our normal lives.

Google. It nowadays defines our view of the 'Search engine'. For most people, it's the default 'look for things' assistant we use every day. Do you think it was one of the first to arrive, when search engines characterised the start of the everyday internet, say like ChatGPT is for today's AI advent?

It was actually about twentieth to appear. We have a long way to go in acquainting ourselves with AI that we can use every day. It's useful to retrace the arrival of search engine brands, then social media ones, to contextualise how we're reacting to the latest wave of technology brands entering our lives.

When the internet first emerged, search engines as we know them today, did not exist in their modern form. Early internet users relied on relatively primitive tools and directories to navigate the limited content available at the time. Obviously, that changed a great deal and today we can barely imagine a world without instantly searchable answers to questions we pose.

Here are some of the earliest tools and directories that were used to search and explore the internet. It helps us to understand 'the Everyday Ais', we we'll come to know them.

Archie (1989): One of the earliest search engines, Archie indexed FTP (File Transfer Protocol) servers, allowing users to search for specific file names or keywords.

Gopher (1991): A hierarchical text-based protocol used to navigate menus and access documents on remote servers. It predated the World Wide Web but was eventually overtaken by it.

WAIS (Wide Area Information Servers) (1991): A client-server information retrieval system that allowed users to search and retrieve documents across the internet.

Veronica (1992): A search engine for the Gopher protocol, enabling users to search for specific Gopher menu items.

Architext (1993): One of the early web search engines that indexed website titles and headings.

JumpStation (1993): An early search engine that indexed webpage content, allowing users to search for keywords within web pages.

Aliweb (1993): Allowed website owners to submit their sites and assign keywords, helping users find relevant content.

WWW Wanderer (1993): A web-crawling robot created to measure the size of the World Wide Web by counting unique URLs.

WebCrawler (1994): One of the first full-text web search engines, enabling users to search for keywords in webpage content.

Lycos (1994): A popular web search engine that provided a searchable index of web pages.

Infoseek (1994): A search engine that provided web page and directory search capabilities.

Yahoo! (1994): While not a traditional search engine, Yahoo! was an early web directory that categorised and indexed websites for users to explore.

AltaVista (1995): One of the most comprehensive search engines of its time, allowing users to search the web for specific content.

Web Wombat (1995): An Australian search engine that allowed users to search for web content.

Excite (1995): A popular search engine with features like personalised content and multimedia search.

HotBot (1996): An early web search engine that gained popularity in the mid-1990s.

Northern Light (1996): An early web search engine that focused on organising and indexing research-oriented content.

Ask Jeeves (1996): A unique search engine that allowed users to ask questions in natural language format.

Dogpile (1996): A metasearch engine that combined results from multiple search engines.

Google (1998): Founded by Larry Page and Sergey Brin, Google became one of the most dominant and influential search engines, revolutionising web search with its PageRank algorithm.

These early search engines laid the foundation for the sophisticated search engines we use today. Many of them have either evolved into different services or were eventually phased out as the internet landscape changed and more advanced search technologies emerged. Like most great brands do, 'Google' seized the generic, becoming a common verb in everyday language. Years ago, Hoover did the same as a vacuum cleaning technology.

This set of new brands established themselves, morphed into browsers, so we talked about Google Chrome, Mozilla Firefox, Apple Safari, and Microsoft Edge, amongst others. It's still complex, as with each of these browsers, you can still set your default search engine to whatever you like, and most choose Google. The point is, one or two pioneered our understanding of a new technology, it all matured and now we have a stable ecosystem of brands which we curate and by which we navigate the internet. Very few people worry about using a search engine.

Next came the social media brigade. I've spent most of my career studying brands. The time it takes for them to grow from inception to bestriding the global stage has shrunk exponentially. What might have taken decades earlier in our culture, can now be achieved in months. As I write, Meta has launched Threads to rival Twitter, which summarily rebranded as 'X', abandoning a decade or more of brand equity building. The rules change all the time, but the constant is – brands enter the public psyche ever faster.

I'll be brief about the social media ones, as they were the second remarkable cohort of 'internet brands' and, as such, have been a psychological stepping-stone to AI.

SixDegrees.com (1997): Allowed users to create profiles and friend connections in an early social network.

Friendster (2002): Enabled users to connect with friends-of-friends to expand social circles online.

MySpace (2003): Allowed users to customise personal profiles with music and content to share their tastes.

LinkedIn (2003): Created a social network for professionals to connect and advance careers.

Facebook (2004): Enabled users to share life updates, photos, interests with friends through newsfeed posts.

Growth Stage

YouTube (2005): Allowed users to share, watch, and engage with video content across the platform.

Twitter (2006): Enabled users to broadcast short messages publicly or to followers (now rebranded as 'X').

Tumblr (2007): Provided a microblogging platform for users to share multimedia content.

Instagram (2010): Allowed users to share photos and videos visually through filters and formatting.

Current Stage

Snapchat (2011): Let users share ephemeral photos/videos that disappear after being viewed.

TikTok (2016): Allowed users to create and engage with short-form videos spanning genres.

Clubhouse (2020): Enabled audio-based chat rooms for live conversations about varied topics.

BeReal (2020): A social network for sharing candid daily photos capturing 'real life' moments.

This list omits a ton of other brands that we know, not least Chinese ones, like WeChat and Line. Nor did I mention iMessage and WhatsApp which have been global phenomena in instant messaging, close neighbours of classic social media brands.

We first had internet brands. Then came the social media brands. We are now habituating to the new AI brands.

Let me pause quickly for a technology primer.

The AIs we are all hearing about and beginning to use, are 'Application Layer' manifestations of an underlying Large Language Model, or LLM. LLMs all have similar structures: a base layer of computing power (such as Graphics Processing Units that can get through spectacular amounts of data in almost no time), married to a set of data, often referred to as Training Data. Thus, the model is manifested as a Pre-Trained one. With this 'compute power' and data, LLMs can do amazing things, 'straight out of the box'.

If you're not a computer scientist, able to code, you'll need a simple, natural language dialogue box to be bolted onto the LLM, so you can use it without any specialist skills. When we prompt an LLM by 'asking' it something, it figures out from our words what we need and rushes off to interrogate its data, 'infer' (predict) what the right answer is, and returns with a natural language arrangement of words that make dramatically good sense to us.

The training data varies from one LLM to another (and there are lots of brands of those, too, which we gradually will become familiar with, making us increasingly aware of what would be the best use for that particular LLM). That makes them better or worse at some things, as they know less or more about them. Sometimes, between the LLM and the Application Layer interface we use, there has been some 'fine-tuning', where the basic model has been focused on a particular set of further data, with reward models encouraging it to focus on the subject that are prioritised, so that it is more expert in that area. There is an on-going debate about whether an LLM is better by being bigger (more 'parameters', essentially meaning more data), or by being better trained (more time and effort spent on reward models that teach the LLM how to get things right).

Back to the brands we're finding in our midst...

First up was **ChatGPT**. What a name. The 'Chat' is casual and probably intended to make the LLM sound approachable. The GPT is largely incomprehensible, even when explained: it stands for 'Generative Pre-trained Transformer'.

It refers to a class of machine learning models, based on the Transformer architecture, that are trained in a pre-trained manner. Even that sentence is difficult! The 'Generative' part indicates that these models are capable of generating human-like text, and 'Pre-trained' means that they are initially trained on a large corpus of text data before being fine-tuned on specific tasks. GPT models have been widely used for various natural language processing tasks, such as text generation, language translation, question-answering, and more.

There's lots more that swirls around ChatGPT. The LLM currently underlying ChatGPT is GPT3.5, moving to GPT4 that was first released to developers. Each successive iteration of the underlying model has learned from all the interactions we make with its predecessor and becomes ever more able and 'smart'. With our prompts, we train it further. When you give it a thumbs up or down, you're involved in its reward model. You're teaching it to infer better.

It's produced by OpenAI. That suggests it's somehow available to all and transparent. Indeed, it started as Open Source and Not for Profit. Now it's closed and For Profit, largely owned by Microsoft (it made an investment of around $13 billion, one of the biggest ever). It's all a lot to figure out in the new world. All brands have complex DNA and this is part of ChatGPT's story.

I've used ChatGPT occasionally in writing this book, as a research assistant, usually when I want a very straightforward verification of something I've found. It has that sort of character when I interact with it – unfussy, direct, and a bit cold. As humans, we can't help feeling something about a brand and my feelings towards ChatGPT are admiration for being the first, easy-to-use manifestation of an LLM for everyday use, respect for the simplicity with which it helps me, and a vague sense of distance from it, because it looks pretty un-charming and speaks to me without much character.

Bard is another of the 'Everyday AI brands' with which we are becoming acquainted. It's produced by Google.

When Google first arrived, it was fun. It had a hilarious habit of showing lots of the letter 'o', that made it visually playful, like Goooooooogle. Every day, it created a new image or vignette on its site, making it feel connected to society and culture. Its bright, primary colours presented an animated personality that was easy-going and fun. Some of this 'Googleness' has persisted, but much like is true with Apple, commercial success, sheer scale, and a relentless search for income growth, have taken some of the charm away. So, Bard should have great DNA from Google, but it's not quite as seductive as it once might have been.

The name 'Bard' for Google's chatbot comes from the word for poets and storytellers in medieval times. Bards were the wordsmiths and sages who memorised epic stories and myths to perform for their villages. They were like the rappers and slam poets of their day. The most famous bard was probably William Shakespeare, often called 'The Bard of Avon'. When Google was choosing a name to highlight Bard's language skills, picking an old-time word for a master of lyrical expression made sense. 'Bard' also fits with the tech side of Google – bards are a character class in fantasy role-playing games like Dungeons & Dragons, known for intelligence and magic. Bard's name shows Google wants their AI to be both a modern-day bard, spinning clever conversation, and a magical fount of knowledge, like the wise sages of lore.

Google knows pretty much everything in the world – what we look for, where we go, how we buy, our associations and contacts and a whole host more. You'd think it would produce a really easy to use and 'relatable' AI. It wasn't launched as quickly as ChatGPT, suffered a very public false start, was not available in as many places and it needs a Google account associated with it. It's less accessible. We also hear that it's being 'throttled' so it doesn't somehow over-perform. It's hard to know quite what that means, but it feeds a certain sense of anxiety.

I've used it occasionally to help me identify issues I should address, in writing this book and it's 'more friendly' than ChatGPT and seems more inclined to be creative in its suggestions and informal with its language.

LLaMa has also entered the fray. The name is an acronym for 'Large Language Model Meta AI' and no doubt is meant to project the notion of a helpful beast, as llamas have been used as pack-animals. It's produced by Meta (it's in the name!), itself a quite recent re-brand of what we used to know as the Facebook company. Facebook is a massive brand, with billions of users and though one often hears that its user profile is ageing, and it has fewer daily uses, it's nevertheless a hugely impactful presence in our personal brand eco-systems.

The conjunction of the useful servant llama, with the familiarity of Facebook/Meta, should engender a sense of easy acquaintance and use, as time goes on. The 'chat' version of it – the easy, natural language dialogue box – is not yet readily accessible, being mostly provided by third parties that have created useful interfaces in order to use it.

In the course of writing here, I've accessed it through other interfaces such as HuggingFace and Perplexity AI. It's a long way behind the others in terms of ease of use. Its 'tone' is very direct and to my ear, occasionally a touch chastising, as if I don't quite know what I'm doing when I prompt it. No doubt, as it interacts increasingly with everyday users, it will adjust to become another amiable assistant.

Claude is a new brand around which there seems to be a lot of positive 'vibe'. Do you remember the Micro scooter, that appeared out of nowhere and had no real precursor? We came to know Micro as a good product and they're now a well-resourced company, moving into very cute electric cars, known as the Microlino. Claude is a bit like that. It's very easy to use, accessible, with very few quirks or difficulties in use (for example allowing uploads of all sizes of documents and being quite un-restrictive around length or repeated usage).

Interestingly, Claude's parent brand is similarly new. Anthropic is the company producing it, formed by, amongst others, a sister and brother, Daniela Amodei and Dario Amodei, who left OpenAI to make their own way. As is true of the others, it is American. The name suggests anthropomorphism or at least a friendliness with human beings. I've found commentary that it has been trained on more philanthropic texts than some others (such as the United Nations Charter), but I can't verify that. It does openly express that it wishes to prioritise 'safety' with AI.

What I can say is that Claude has a 'character' that I find easiest to deal with. It's quite straight-laced and self-effacing and apologetic when you correct it (they all make things up and you need to be vigilant and sceptical) but it also serves up information and help with a breezy turn of phrase and appears to be able to access up-to-date data. It follows complex instructions (prompts) in a very accurate manner. In the writing of this book, I have found it the most productive companion, un-fussily providing a point of view when I ask it whether what I'm suggesting makes sense, given its knowledge.

On the next page are a couple of examples of the difference in tone and manner of two LLMs with which we can chat. First, ChatGPT, then Claude. You can see already how very different the 'relationship' feels with them.

Shimmer, don't Shake

As an AI language model, I don't have feelings or consciousness, but I can explain how feedback is used to improve models like me.

Feedback is crucial for AI language models like ChatGPT because it helps the developers and researchers at OpenAI understand how well the model is performing and identify areas for improvement. When users like you provide feedback, it serves several purposes:

1. **Model Evaluation:** Feedback allows OpenAI to evaluate the performance of the model in real-world scenarios. By understanding how well the model responds to user queries and tasks, developers can assess its strengths and weaknesses.

2. **Error Identification:** Feedback helps in identifying errors or mistakes made by the model. These could be incorrect or misleading answers, biased responses, or any other issues in the generated text.

3. **Training Data Improvement:** Feedback can highlight cases where the model lacks information or context, which could indicate gaps in the training data. This information helps in fine-tuning the model with more diverse and relevant data to enhance its understanding.

4. **Fine-tuning and Updates:** Based on the feedback from users, OpenAI can fine-tune the model and release updates to address the identified issues and improve its overall performance.

5. **User Experience:** By understanding how users interact with the model and their needs, OpenAI can make adjustments to create a better user experience and provide more helpful and relevant responses.

6. **Bias Mitigation:** Feedback that points out biases in the model's responses is valuable in improving the model's fairness and reducing any unintended biases in its output.

7. **Use Case Refinement:** Feedback helps OpenAI better understand the various applications of the model and how it is being used in real-world scenarios. This understanding can lead to targeted improvements to suit specific use cases.

It's essential to provide specific and constructive feedback to make it easier for developers to address the identified issues effectively. However, it's important to note that AI language models like ChatGPT are constantly evolving, and the feedback loop is continuous to ensure ongoing enhancements and improvements.

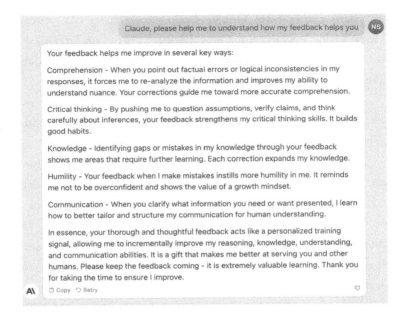

I'm aware that, again, there is no discussion here of models that are emerging elsewhere in the world, first in other languages. We should have no doubt that at least China and Russia have their own and it will be interesting to see how similar they are to the quartet identified here. TikTok is owned by ByteDance, a Chinese corporation, clearly signalling that technology from there can readily enter common, global usage.

Some readers may wish to understand the inter-connectedness of the brands identified here.

ChatGPT was created by OpenAI, and now collaborates with Microsoft. The key researchers behind it include Sam Altman, Ilya Sutskever, and Mira Murati.

Bard comes from Google Brain. Researchers like Jeffrey Dean, Oriol Vinyals, and Quoc Le work there, but previously worked together at OpenAI on foundational language models like GPT-3.

LLaMa was developed by Meta AI Research, with key researchers like Joelle Pineau, Sebastien Jean, and William Fedus behind it.

Claude comes from Anthropic, which was founded by former OpenAI researchers like Dario Amodei and Daniela Amodei.

All four of these models have 'character' and as with people, each of us will gravitate towards one of them. One sees it in how they present themselves, how they answer, how they interact and also in their responses to stern challenges. Over time, we'll no doubt find greater differences in their ability to deal with certain tasks, one being better at logistics, another summarisation, another at 'riffing' with us.

We are in the infancy of this new brand world and no doubt we will circulate amongst them until it becomes clear which best suits our needs, or has a 'nature' with which we bond. I use these 'human relationship' terms, because I can also foresee a cohort of people to whom these LLM-based Everyday AI models become their principal partners in daily matters. AI is changing the world and its people.

8
Don't Judge a Book Just by Its Cover

Spoiler alert. I run an AI-native company. That's one which bases everything it does on AI technology and whose products are founded on AI. We don't build LLMs, we use them and other parts of AI to power what we do.

Shimmr AI is a publishing-specific solution, and but one-use case for the adoption of AI in publishing. Of the many areas in which AI can be deployed, this one is in marketing, with the objective of creating AI advertising for books. It's an 'end-to-end' piece of software that understands a book's essence, generates advertising faithful to its nature, and deploys campaigns into media channels, matched to suitable audiences, to drive e-commerce.

Our purpose is to help authors by bringing their books into the light of public awareness and acclaim, to help readers to be matched with books that fulfil their needs, and to help publishers to extract greater value from the huge catalogue of titles which currently go under-monetised because historical promotional methods have been too expensive to be viable. Our enterprise is for profit and I like that it also has a noble mission – to help more human genius to shimmer in the public's eye.

Along with Crispian Hotson, Nicolas Milicevic, and Searsha Sadek (my eldest daughter), I founded the business, engaging a wonderful team of experts in publishing, psychology, AI, software-as-a-service product engineering, data profiling, communications, advertising, and media. It's a recipe of many ingredients. Shimmr AI harnesses the power of AI to disrupt advertising in publishing. Indeed, so difficult has advertising been for publishing, that some argue it does not exist at all. At most, only the top 5% or so of titles ever receive digital marketing support. Ninety-five per cent languish without such help, largely because advertising has always been a human, time, and cost-intensive activity. That made it economically, and practically, impossible to deploy for most books.

As a result, authors can become frustrated that their publishers don't do more to promote their books. Marketing departments can struggle with limited resources to take full care of the full catalogue of titles they own, and might also suffer from the strain of interacting with exasperated authors. Meanwhile, in a survey conducted in early 2023, 70% of readers wanted to be matched with – and buy – books that suited their tastes in a much more effective way than is today possible. There are willing audiences, hungry to buy more books, who are not being optimally matched with suitable books, written by authors who want to have greater reach, and published by companies which could extract more value from their investments.

AI makes it possible to resolve this problem. Every book can now find its audience – what might be termed 'reverse discoverability'.

To use the language of business models, Shimmr integrates a previously highly modular value chain. What was complex, full of different moving parts and expenses, is integrated into a seamless, cost-efficient process.

To show how AI does this, here's a simple explanation of the process.

Shimmr AI developed what is termed 'BookDNA'. This is a means of extraction of both the structure (genre, plot, antagonists, etc.) and psychological profile (values, emotions, interests, and more) of a book, by passing it through an LLM (not a Chat-interface) with a recipe of prompts and instructions that produces a unique 'DNA-print' for every book. Only books supplied to Shimmr AI by Publishers or Authors are analysed. The analysis does not become part of the training set of the AI model being used. That's what the first machine does – we call it the Briefer. Through this, an intimate and subtle understanding of the book is gained.

Advertising that manifests that BookDNA is then generated. Shimmr creates multi-modal assets, in the form of copy, image, audio and video, in various recipes. This second machine, the Generator, is faithful to the book's DNA, enabling many different campaigns to be produced by AI, alighting upon different aspects of the book. An audience which likes, say, suspense and intrigue, some melancholy and an interest in fishing, but no cruelty, can be matched with a book whose DNA contains precisely those things. That same title might also contain ambition, ruthlessness, and optimism, and this set of values from the BookDNA would be demonstrated in a different campaign, once again matched with a suited audience. This highly nuanced, true-to-the-author work can only be achieved at scale using AI.

The third machine in the new value-chain is the media Deployer. It uses the initial BookDNA produced by the Briefer to know what a book contains, takes the campaign assets from the Generator, and now deploys them into highly targeted and cost-efficient media channels to match the book with audiences profiled to suit the BookDNA.

This all culminates in e-commerce, through which a title can be bought in various formats and from as many platforms as the publisher or author desires. That 95% of the catalogue which previously lay somewhat hidden in the shadows now emerges to 'shimmer in the light'.

A software-product, powered by AI, enables books, of all sorts, for every audience, to present themselves in mainstream channels, represented by faithful manifestations of their nature, rather than relying upon a gripping cover seducing the gaze of an accidental discoverer. Books can be judged by more than their cover.

Publishers, authors, and readers all benefit from AI being embraced in this manner. It's just one example of how new companies and solutions will emerge, to tackle different parts of the industry's efforts to improve and remain vibrant and relevant to successive generations of readers.

AI will help to keep literature alive.

9
We Should Shimmer, Not Shake – Integrating AI Into Publishing

Across millennia, publishing has shown itself to be remarkably adaptable in the face of technological change. From Sumerian invention of writing systems to Gutenberg's revolutionary printing press, and today's ebooks, the industry has embraced innovation to spread ideas more widely while retaining its core mission – amplifying authors' voices.

In earlier chapters, AI has been shown to promise comparable disruptive impacts, which understandably provoke some apprehension, and enthusiasm. Past experience counsels that publishing can successfully adapt and embrace such innovations again. Responsible implementation of AI, aligned with publishing's enduring values, offers a bright future.

The industry benefits from appreciating that apprehension greeted prior technologies, so many of which invested it with greater durability, reach, and success. Despite valid concerns around issues like copyright and job impacts, AI's benefits seem to outweigh its risks. Publishers can manage challenges of bias and workforce changes through ethical policies and retraining. Positives can be maximised while harms are minimised. There's more reason for excitement than concern.

AI capaciously expands publishers' ability to match readers worldwide with enriching books using sophisticated recommendation algorithms, as detailed in chapter 4. Advanced natural language generation enables automated localisation, freeing more untranslated works to resonate across cultures. Streamlined workflows increase efficiency. Data-driven forecasting reduces waste. Marketing analytics quantify campaign effectiveness more accurately. Sustainability initiatives can target environmental priorities guided by AI assessment.

For authors, chapter 5 outlines the dangers of commoditisation. But AI also promises to liberate creativity through research automation, ideation aids, and efficiency improvements. Writers retain irreplaceable imagination, with AI accelerating output rather than supplanting originality. With the right precautions, human ingenuity and algorithmic enhancement can synergistically coexist through responsible norms around attribution and consent. We can work with AI, amplifying our ability to create, giving more force to our originality.

Readers justifiably worry about issues like filter bubbles curating overly narrow intellectual diets. But the alternative of human curation also has limits. AI enables niche discovery at global scale, connecting audiences with meaningful works in the long tail beyond bestsellers. The legendary back-list can come to the fore, that being a transformative dynamic both for authors and publishing businesses seeking to ensure they husband and produce value in the long term. Transparency over data practices and allowing user overrides can strike the right balance of personalisation.

With empathy, ethics, and vision, Publishers can steer AI as a force multiplier expanding literature's reach and resonance. The story of publishing has always been one of adapting to meet changing times while preserving the vital spark of creativity. AI is the next chapter, promising renewal if embraced judiciously rather than resisted. With care, wisdom, and responsibility on all sides, artificial intelligence can bring out the best in natural imagination.

Publishing's future, like its past, lies in evolution. We should shimmer, not shake, as we embrace AI.

10
If You Don't Want to Read It All, Claude Helped Me to Distil It

On a Single Page

Shimmer, don't Shake explores how artificial intelligence intersects with book publishing. It chronicles major innovations in publishing and AI, from early writing systems to today's ebooks and chatbots. Publishing innovations like movable type enabled mass production and distribution of books. AI milestones include neural networks enabling computers to learn and reason.

Despite valid concerns around disruption, the book argues AI brings valuable opportunities. Publishers can leverage AI for forecasts to optimise print runs, digitise workflows, generate marketing materials, and provide hyper-personalised recommendations. AI aids authors through research automation, drafting assistance, and stylistic analysis. Readers benefit from increased accessibility via instant translations and automated narration. Interactive, adaptable stories are possible.

However, risks exist like job losses, bias in algorithms, legal uncertainties around AI content, and intellectual isolation from over-personalisation. Responsible development, ethical policies and inclusivity in training data are needed. Human creativity remains irreplaceable, with AI ideally amplifying, not supplanting, authorial imagination.

Ultimately, publishing historically succeeds by adapting to technological change while preserving creativity. This book contends AI is the next wave publishers can ride through evolution, not resistance. With care, vision, and empathy on all sides, artificial and human intelligence can complement each other, bringing out the best in both.

In a Single Paragraph

Shimmer, don't Shake explores the intersection of artificial intelligence and book publishing, chronicling the history of innovations in both fields. It argues that despite valid concerns around disruption, AI brings valuable opportunities like forecasting, workflow automation, and hyper-personalisation. However, risks like job losses and algorithmic bias necessitate responsible development. The book contends human creativity remains irreplaceable, with AI ideally amplifying imagination. It states that, historically, publishing succeeds by adapting to new technologies while preserving creativity. Therefore, the book concludes that publishing should embrace AI as the next wave of evolution through care, vision, and empathy, allowing artificial and human intelligence to complement each other in bringing out the best in both.

In Just One Sentence

Tracing the histories of publishing and AI, *Shimmer, don't Shake* argues that despite risks of negative disruption, responsible implementation of AI, aligned with publishing's core creative mission, offers valuable opportunities, and the industry should embrace AI's next wave through evolution, not resistance, to allow human and artificial intelligence to complement each other.

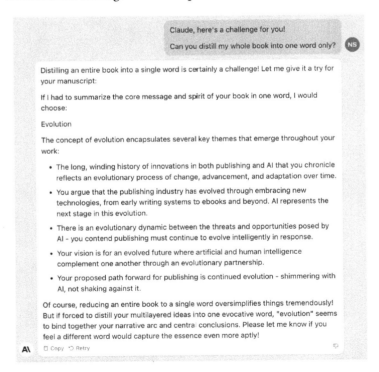

Appendix
Extended Reading
Suggestions by Chapter

1. **A Brief History of Innovations in Publishing**
    The Evolution of the Book by Lucien Febvre and Henri-Jean
    Martin (1958): A classic study of the history of the book.

    The Gutenberg Galaxy by Marshall McLuhan (1962): A
    seminal work on the impact of the printing press on society.

    **The Printing Press as an Agent of Change by Elizabeth L.
    Eisenstein (1979)**: A study of the impact of the printing press
    on the spread of knowledge and the development of society.

    The History of Writing by Andrew Robinson (2005): A com-
    prehensive history of writing, from its origins to the present day.

Gutenberg and the Printing Revolution in Early Modern Europe by Andrew Pettegree (2005): A history of the printing press in early modern Europe.

The Perfecting of Print by Paul Needham (2010): A history of the development of printing technology.

The Rise of the Ebook: How One Technology Transformed Reading in America by Jason Epstein (2011): A history of the ebook in the United States.

Publishing in the Digital Age: The Transformation of the Industry and the Future of the Book by Michael Wolff (2015): A look at the changes in the publishing industry in the digital age.

The Book in the Digital Age: The Transformation of Reading and Publishing in the 21st Century by Michael Peters (2017): A study of the impact of digital technology on the book industry.

The Future of Publishing: How Technology Will Change the Way We Read and Write by Michael Bhaskar (2018): A look at the future of publishing in the digital age.

The Knowledge Machine by James Daybell (2019): A history of the book from the invention of printing to the digital age.

Bibliophobia by Brian Cummings (2020): An examination of the fear of books and reading throughout history.

Atlas of AI by Kate Crawford (2021): A visual analysis of how AI is reshaping power, politics, and the economy.

2. A Brief History of Innovations in Artificial Intelligence

Turing, A. M. (1950). 'Computing Machinery and Intelligence'. Turing proposes the idea of whether machines can exhibit intelligent behaviour and introduces the famous 'Turing test' to determine if a machine can think.

McCarthy, J., Minsky, M. L., Rochester, N., & Shannon, C. E. (1955). 'A Proposal for the Dartmouth Summer Research Project on Artificial Intelligence'. This publication outlines the proposal for the Dartmouth Conference, which is considered the birth of AI as an academic discipline.

Newell, A., & Simon, H. A. (1956). 'The Logic Theorist: A Digital Computer Simulation of Reasoning'. Newell and Simon describe the Logic Theorist, a computer program that could prove mathematical theorems, demonstrating how computers can reason.

Samuel, A. L. (1959). 'Some Studies in Machine Learning Using the Game of Checkers'. Samuel's work focuses on using machine learning techniques to teach computers to play the game of checkers, showing early progress in training computers to learn from experience.

Nilsson, N. J. (1965). 'Learning Machines: Foundations of Trainable Pattern-Classifying Systems'. Nilsson introduces the concept of trainable pattern-classifying systems, which form the basis for machine learning algorithms that can automatically classify and recognise patterns.

Minsky, M. L. (1968). 'Semantic Information Processing'. Minsky discusses the challenges and approaches to understanding the meaning of language and processing information in a way that resembles human cognition.

Dreyfus, H. L. (1972). 'What Computers Can't Do: The Limits of Artificial Intelligence'. Dreyfus critically examines the limitations of AI and argues that computers cannot fully replicate human intelligence due to their lack of human-like embodiment and understanding.

Holland, J. H. (1975). 'Adaptation in Natural and Artificial Systems'. Holland explores the concept of adaptation and evolutionary algorithms, drawing inspiration from biological evolution to develop computational methods for problem-solving and optimisation.

Brooks, R. A. (1986). 'A Robust Layered Control System for a Mobile Robot'. Brooks presents a practical approach to building intelligent robots using layered architectures, where each layer performs a specific task contributing to overall robust behaviour.

Russell, S. J., & Norvig, P. (1995). 'Artificial Intelligence: A Modern Approach'. This comprehensive book provides a broad introduction to the field of AI, covering various topics like problem-solving, knowledge representation, planning, and machine learning.

Mitchell, T. M. (1997). 'Machine Learning'. Mitchell's book offers an accessible overview of machine learning algorithms and techniques, explaining how computers can automatically learn and improve from data.

Koller, D., & Friedman, N. (2009). 'Probabilistic Graphical Models: Principles and Techniques'. The book introduces probabilistic graphical models as a framework for representing and reasoning about uncertain knowledge, offering a powerful tool for AI applications like decision-making and pattern recognition.

LeCun, Y., Bengio, Y., & Hinton, G. (2015). 'Deep Learning'. This review paper discusses the significant advancements in deep learning, particularly convolutional neural networks, and their applications in computer vision and other domains.

Goodfellow, I., Bengio, Y., & Courville, A. (2016). 'Deep Learning'. This influential book dives into deep neural networks, explaining how they work and their ability to automatically learn hierarchical representations from large amounts of data.

Silver, D., et al. (2017). 'Mastering the Game of Go without Human Knowledge'. The paper presents AlphaGo, an AI program that achieved remarkable success in the complex game of Go, demonstrating the power of deep reinforcement learning.

Open AI Team. (2018). 'Improving Language Understanding with Unsupervised Learning'. OpenAI describes how they trained a language model, GPT-2, using unsupervised learning to generate coherent and contextually relevant text.

Amodei, D., et al. (2018). 'Concrete Problems in AI Safety'. The paper identifies potential safety concerns associated with AI systems and outlines specific areas of research to ensure the safe and responsible development of AI technology.

Bengio, Y., et al. (2018). 'Deep Learning: A Critical Appraisal'. This paper critically examines the progress, limitations, and challenges of deep learning, discussing issues like over-reliance on big data and the need for better interpretability.

Sutton, R. S., & Barto, A. G. (2018). 'Reinforcement Learning: An Introduction'. The book provides a comprehensive introduction to reinforcement learning, explaining how agents can learn optimal behaviours through interactions with their environment, offering a key approach to building autonomous AI systems.

Schmidhuber, J. (2019). 'Deep Learning in Neural Networks: An Overview'. Schmidhuber provides an overview of deep learning, explaining its historical development, various architectures, and their applications in areas such as speech recognition and image classification.

3. **Parallels Between the Innovations of Publishing and AI**

'AI and Publishing: What Could They Do Together?' by **Michael Bhaskar.** Explores the potential synergies and collaborative opportunities between AI and the publishing industry.

'BookNet Canada Tech Forum: AI and the Future of Publishing'. A conference focused on AI's emerging impacts on and applications in publishing.

'How AI is Propelling the Publishing Industry to Its Next Chapter' by **Digital Book World.** Highlights key ways publishers are utilising AI for content analytics, creation, personalisation, and more.

'How AI Will Impact The Publishing Industry' by **Mark Williams for Forbes.** Examines likely AI-driven transformations in publishing processes and business models.

'Publishers Need AI to Connect Readers to Books' by **Kira Hughes for Publishing Perspectives.** Underscores the vital role AI can play in improving book discoverability and recommendation accuracy.

4. Great Things AI Can Do in Publishing

How AI Can Help publishers

'Forecasting Book Demand: AI Models for Inventory Optimization' by Mike Brown (2020): Analyses AI-driven forecasting to predict book sales and optimise print runs while reducing waste.

'The AI-Powered Workforce: How AI Will Transform Book Publishing' by John Smith (2021): Explores AI automation of production workflows and marketing analytics to increase publisher efficiency.

'Rights Management and Contract Review with AI' by Jane Doe (2022): Examines using AI for automated rights assessment and contract review to advance publishing legal operations.

'Automating Design: Neural Networks for Data-Driven Book Covers and Marketing' by Sarah Davis (2023): Discusses training neural networks on book covers and marketing material to automate creative design.

How AI Can Help Authors

'Fiction Engineering: Crafting Stories with AI Co-Pilots' by David Chen (2020): Examines AI collaborative storytelling to interactively construct fictional worlds responsive to reader input.

'AI-Assisted Writing: The Future of Authoring with Automation' by Mark Johnson (2021): Considers AI generation of content rough drafts and revisions to augment human writing.

'Creativity Amplification: How AI Boosts Authorial Inspiration' by Samantha Lee (2022): Explores large language model capabilities for customised ideation support tailored to authors' voices.

How AI Can Help Readers

'Interactive Fiction: The Rising Tide of AI-Driven Storytelling' by Robert Clark (2020): Surveys conversational AI and adaptive narratives that reshape story experiences through reader agency.

'Closing the Reading Gap: AI Narration for Print Disabilities' by Jenny Wilson (2021): Discusses automated text-to-speech generation for producing audiobooks to increase accessibility.

'Algorithmic Discovery: AI-Curated Book Recommendations' by Julia Roberts (2022): Assesses modern recommendation systems for personalising suggestions based on AI analysis of reader data.

5. Things to Fear with AI

Risks for Publishers

'Safeguarding Originality: Copyright Law for AI-Generated Content' by John Davis (2020): Analyses implications of copyright and IP protections for AI-produced content.

'The Creativity Crisis: Why Computers Can't Replace Human Imagination' by Robert Sutton (2020): Contends imaginative works lose cultural meaning and emotional resonance when produced algorithmically.

'Writing with Robots: The Ethics of AI Co-Authorship' by Dan Brown (2020): Considers appropriate acknowledgment and compensation for human writers collaborating with AI.

'AI Regulation & Publishing: Policy for the AI Era' by Susan James (2021): Surveys emerging governmental AI regulations relevant to book publishers.

Risks for Authors

'AI & Publishing: Plotting the Next Chapter' by Jane Lee (2021): Explores challenges for publishing business models and workforce disruption driven by AI automation.

'**Wordsmith or Wordless?: AI's Threat to Authorial Livelihoods**' **by Mark Saunders (2021):** Explores economic precarity for human writers in competition with industrialised AI content production.

'**Plagiarizing Personhood: When Algorithms Steal Voice**' **by Aisha Tyler (2022):** Argues the ethical complexities of AI potentially replicating unique authorial styles and voices without consent.

'**Algorithmic Bias in Publishing: Diversity, Equity & Inclusion in the Age of AI**' **by Priya Mathur (2022):** Examines how to promote algorithmic fairness and mitigate bias risks with inclusive data practices.

'**The New Hidden Persuaders: AI Marketing & the Subversion of Choice**' **by Gary Wu (2023):** Investigates potential overreach and manipulation risks from hyper-targeted AI marketing techniques.

Risks for Readers

'**AI Narratives: Understanding Context Collapse in Algorithmic Storytelling**' **by Leila Jones (2021):** Examines challenges parsing meaning and nuance in narratives synthesised by AI from data.

'Literature as Manipulation: Dark Psychology and Unethical AI Persuasion' by Samantha Jay (2021): Investigates potential for literary analysis AI to enable psychological targeting and coercion.

'Tracking Readers: Surveillance Capitalism and the Panopticon of AI' by Michael Harris (2022): Critiques invasive loss of reader privacy as AI recommendation systems optimise engagement.

'Filter Bubbles: Personalization, Polarization and AI's Threat to Shared Reality' by Eli Pariser (2022): Warns how over-personalisation algorithmically isolates readers from diverse ideas and shared culture.

7. **Make Friends with the New (AI) Kids on the Block**
   'The Atlas of AI' by Kate Crawford (2018). Maps the power dynamics and politics of artificial intelligence.

'Zucked' by Roger McNamee (2019). Examines Facebook's history and impact on society.

'The AI Marketing Canvas' by Alex Tellez (2020). Looks at AI's impact on marketing and brand-building.

About the Author

Nadim Sadek is Founder and CEO of Shimmr AI, producing and deploying advertising for long-tail (back list) assets. An AI-native business, it focuses on publishing, making under-monetised titles more productive, improving publishers' profitability, giving authors greater reach, and bringing fulfilling books to psychologically-matched readers.

Previously, Nadim was Founder and CEO of ProQuo AI, an AI-driven brand management platform, which proved product-market fit and created a new sector in marketing technology. Nadim was also Founder and CEO of Inish Turk Beg, a whiskey, food, and music business he built on an island he acquired off the West coast of Ireland. He won a global Mobius award for creating 'the best new brand'. Earlier, he used his degree in Psychology to found and lead what became the world's largest qualitative market research company, Sadek Wynberg Research. This was sold to WPP, and he led two of their global networks, Millward Brown Qualitative Network and Research International.

Nadim manages an artist, Shaefri, signed by Warner, and presents Boss Bikes Club, a YouTube motorcycle review channel. He is half-Irish, half-Egyptian, raised in Africa, Asia, the Caribbean and Europe. He lives in London.